Customize

YOUR KNITTING

Quarto is the authority on a wide range of topics.

Quarto educates, entertains and enriches the lives of our readers—enthusiasts and lovers of hands-on living.

www.QuartoKnows.com

© 2016 Quarto Publishing Group USA Inc.
First published in the United States of America in 2016 by
Creative Publishing international, an imprint of
Quarto Publishing Group USA Inc.
400 First Avenue North
Suite 400
Minneapolis, MN 55401
1-800-328-3895
QuartoKnows.com
Visit our blogs at QuartoKnows.com

10 9 8 7 6 5 4 3 2 1

ISBN: 978-1-58923-886-2

Digital edition published in 2016
eISBN: 978-1-63159-150-1

Library of Congress Cataloging-in-Publication Data available

Design and page layout: Laura McFadden Design, Inc.
Cover Image: Shutterstock
Photography: Chris Hubert; Glenn Scott Photography
Body Type Illustrations: Sharon Hubert Valencia
Printed in China

ADJUST TO FIT • EMBELLISH TO TASTE

Customize

YOUR KNITTING

Margaret Hubert

Creative Publishing
international

Dedication

To my wonderful family, I could not do any of this without you.

Acknowledgments

It takes a lot of people to put a book together, and this book was particularly challenging because of all the different aspects, from the making of all the garment sections, the photography, the editing, and all the behind the scenes staff. I owe special thanks to:

Lion Brand Yarn Company, who generously contributed the yarn for all the garments and all the step-outs in the book.

Chris Hubert, my son, who did most of the photography, working with me every week for months.

Rita Greenfeder, for her wonderful tech editing skills and diagrams.

Singer Sewing Machine Company, who provided their handy, adjustable dress form, an invaluable tool when making garments.

Guardian Custom Products for providing their E-Z Blocking Board. Every knitter should own one of these.

I also would like to thank **Paula Alexander, Jeannine Buehler, Mary Ann Ciccarone, Adrienne Cooper, Theresa DeLaBarrera, Ginger Dutton, Mary O'Hara, Deb Seda-Testut, Nancy Smith,** and **Marie Stewart** who helped knit all the beautiful garments and **Sharon Hubert Valencia,** who created the body type illustrations and helped with a lot of the finishing.

Heartfelt thanks to my editor and friend **Linda Neubauer.**

Customi Knitting

Professional Finishes

Stylish Embellishments

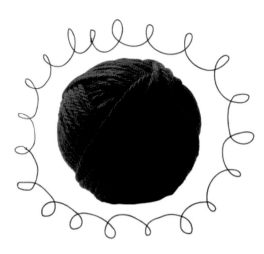

INTRODUCTION

Most patterns in books and magazines are designed to fit the Classic Rectangle body shape, because almost half of all women fit this body type. In the first section of this book, Customize the Fit, you will find instructions for four different sweaters. Each sweater uses a different stitch pattern, and each stitch pattern has a different degree of difficulty. The original instructions are written to fit the Classic Rectangle body type, and guidance is given for how to adjust the patterns to fit different body types. Once you learn the concept, you can apply it to most patterns. The examples in this book are both cardigans and pullovers. Whatever your size, whatever your body type, the most flattering garments are those that fit you properly. In the section Professional Finishes, you will learn methods for finishing your projects that will give them a neat, flawless look. Aside from the fit, there are often features in patterns that we might like to change or details we might like to add. In Stylish Embellishments, you'll find ways to embellish your work, add pockets, or change closures to make your projects truly your own creations.

This book is a guide that will help you knit garments to fit your measurements and your style, then expertly finish them so you will be proud to wear them.

Margaret

SECTION

1

Custom Knitting

The one thing that I hear from so many of my students is that they love to knit, but they only make shawls, scarves, baby blankets, baby sweaters, and hats. The main reason is because whenever they try to make a garment for themselves, it never fits properly.

The first step to making a garment that fits is to understand your body type, and in order to do that you must know how to measure your body correctly.

Included in this section are instructions for four different sweaters, arranged in order of difficulty based on the stitch pattern. After the basic instructions for each pattern are instructions for how to increase and decrease the stitch pattern and how to adjust the shape of the sweater to suit different body types. Once you have determined your body type, read through the instructions, choose a project, and pick up your needles. Be patient, check your gauge, and measure often. You can do this!

Understanding Body Types

There are many different body shapes, but most of us fall into one of four main body types.

Classic Rectangle: The hips and chest are balanced and the waist is not deeply defined. This is the most common body type.

TIP *If you are a Rectangle Shape, you may want to give the appearance of a smaller waistline. You can do this by simply decreasing a few stitches at the waist, working for about 2 inches (5 cm), then increasing back to the original stitch count. Another trick for narrowing at the waist is to use smaller needles through this area. This works particularly well if the pattern is a large multiple of stitches and difficult to increase and decrease.*

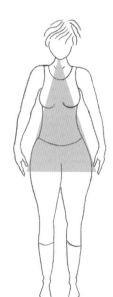

Triangle (sometimes called Pear Shape): The hips are proportionately larger than the chest and shoulders, and the waist is somewhat defined.

TIP *If you are a Triangle Shape, there are a few things that you can do to balance the hip line and smaller chest. You can add small shoulder pads or add interest, such as a ruffle or other embellishment near the neckline, to draw attention upward*

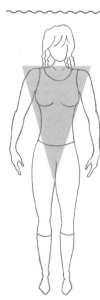

Inverted Triangle: The upper body is proportionately larger with broad shoulders. This body type has an ample chest and wide back, with slim hips.

TIP *If you are an Inverted Triangle, there are a few things that you can do to create balance. You might like to add a V-neck, or add different edges to the bottom of a garment.*

Hourglass: The chest and hips are well balanced and the waist is very defined. The shoulders align with the hips and the upper body is proportionate in length.

TIP *If you are an Hourglass figure, you might want to embrace your curves, and shape the waistline by increasing and decreasing.*

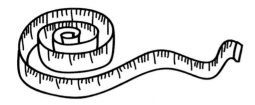

Taking Measurements

Before you begin a project, measure yourself and draw a diagram with your measurements, so that you can readily see where the pattern needs to be adjusted. For example, look at the schematics following the sweater patterns on pages 16, 30, 51, and 66. These show the measurements of the final knitted pieces for each design, assuming one has knit in the correct gauge.

HOW TO MEASURE YOUR BODY

Take your measurements over undergarments for accuracy, using a flexible tape measure. Enlist the help of a friend. When measuring the chest, waist, and hips, make sure to keep the tape measure parallel to the floor all around.

1. Chest/Bust. Place the tape measure under the arms, across the widest part of the back and fullest part of the chest/bust line.

2. Waist. Tie a string or piece of narrow elastic around your middle and allow it to roll to your natural waist-line. Measure at this exact location. Leave the string in place as a reference for measuring the hips and back waist length.

3. Hips. Measure around the fullest part.

4. Back Waist Length. Measure from the prominent bone at the base of the neck down to the waistline string.

5. Cross Back. Measure from one shoulder crest across the back to the other.

6. Sleeve Length. Take two measurements here: With your arm at your side, measure from the shoulder crest to the wrist bone. Then, with your arm slightly away from your body, measure from the armpit to the wrist.

7. Sleeve diameter. Measure around the fullest part of your upper arm.

Adjusting Sleeve Measurements

If you have a slightly wider upper arm measurement than the pattern calls for, there are a few things that you can do to correct the problem.

First, you must determine how the sleeve pattern increases. Generally the increases are about every two inches (five centimeters), gradually shaping from a cuff to the upper arm. If you need more room in the upper arm area, you can make more increases by placing the increase rows closer together, say about every one and one half inch (four centimeters), until you reach the desired width. You will then have to decrease the added stitches in the cap area. The difficulty of the pattern and the multiple of stitches will determine how to make the increases.

Instructions are given for how to make increases and decreases for each of the stitch patterns used in the four designs. If you need to make the sleeves longer or shorter than the pattern calls for, this can also be achieved by changing the spacing between increases.

Little Shells Cardigan

The Little Shell pattern is one of the easiest stitch patterns to adjust for fit. This lovely open fabric not only turns a classic cardigan shape into something special, it works up quickly, has a soft drape, and lends itself to further embellishment.

SKILL LEVEL
EASY

CLASSIC RECTANGLE

Yarn: Light (3)

Shown: Lion Brand Superwash Merino, Color 102 Aqua, 100% Super Wash Merino, 3.5 oz (100 g)/306 yds (280 m): Aqua 5 (5, 6, 7) skeins

Needles: Sizes 4 (3.5 mm) and 6 (4 mm) or size needed to obtain gauge

Gauge: 21 sts and 28 rows = 4" (10 cm) in patt on size 6 needles

20 sts = 4" (10 cm) in seed st on size 4 needles

Take time to check gauge.

Notions:

Seven ½" (1.3 cm) buttons

Stitch markers

Tapestry needle

Sizes: Small (Medium, Large, X-Large)

Finished chest: 34 (38, 42, 46)" [86.5 (96.5, 106.5, 117) cm]

Finished length: 20 (21, 21½, 22½)" [51 (53.5, 54.5, 57) cm]

Note: Pattern is multiple of 7 plus 2.

BACK

With size 4 needles, cast on 86 (100, 114, 128) sts. Work seed st border as follows:

Row 1: *K1, p1, rep from * across row.

Row 2: *P1, k1, rep from * across row. Rep Rows 1 and 2 for 1" (2.5 cm).

Change to size 6 needles and work patt as follows:

Row 1: Knit.

Row 2: Purl.

Row 3: K2, *yo by wrapping yarn over needle to back then to front again, p1, p3tog, p1, yo, k2, rep from * across row.

Row 4: Purl.

Rep Rows 1-4 until piece measures 12½ (13, 13, 13½)" [32 (33, 33, 34.5) cm] from beg, ending with Row 4.

Armhole Shape

Bind off 5 (5, 7, 8) sts at beg of next 2 rows. Making sure to keep patt as established, dec 1 st each side every other row 2 (2, 2, 2) times. Work even in patt on 72 (86, 96, 108) sts until armhole is 7½ (8, 8½, 9)" [19 (20.5, 21.5, 23) cm].

Shoulder Shape

Bind off 20 (24, 26, 28) sts at beg of next 2 rows. Bind off rem 32 (38, 44, 52) sts.

LEFT FRONT

With size 4 needles, cast on 49 (56, 63, 70) sts. Work seed st border as Back. Change to size 6 needles and work as follows:

Row 1: Work Row 1 of patt to last 5 sts, place marker on needle, cont seed st patt on last 5 sts.

Row 2: Work seed st on first 5 sts, patt Row 2 until end of row.

Cont in this manner, keeping 5 sts at Front edge in seed st and rem sts in patt, until 12½ (13, 13, 13½)" [32 (33, 33, 34.5) cm] from beg, ending at arm side.

Armhole Shape

Bind off 5 (5, 7, 8) sts at beg of armhole edge, cont patt to end of row. Making sure to keep patt as established, dec 1 st at armhole side every other row 2 (2, 2, 2) times—42 (49, 54, 60) sts. Keeping Front edge in seed st, cont until armhole is 5½ (6, 6½, 7)" [14 (15, 16.5, 18) cm, ending at Front edge.

Neck Shape

Bind off 19 (21, 24, 28) sts at Front edge, finish row. Making sure to keep patt as established, dec 1 st at neck edge every other row 3 (4, 4, 4) times. Work even on rem 20 (24, 26, 28) sts until armhole is same as Back. Bind off.

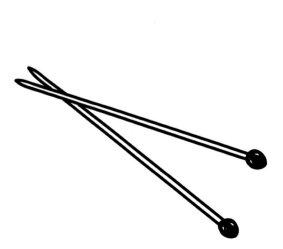

RIGHT FRONT

Before starting Right Front, mark Left Front for 7 buttonholes, evenly spaced, starting at center of bottom seed st border and planning to have the seventh buttonhole added when 1" (2.5 cm) neck border is completed.

With size 4 needles, cast on 49 (56, 63, 70) sts.

Work seed st border as for Back. Change to size 6 needles and work as follows:

Row 1: Work seed st on first 5 sts, place marker, work Row 1 of patt until end of row.

Row 2: Work patt Row 2 to last 5 sts, seed st on last 5 sts.

Cont in this manner, keeping 5 sts at Front edge in seed st, rem sts in patt and working a buttonhole at marked spots as follows (seed st on 2 sts, yo, k2tog, seed on last st) until 12½ (13, 13, 13½)" [32 (33, 33, 34.5) cm from beg, ending at arm side.

Armhole shape

Bind off 5 (5, 7, 8) sts at armhole edge, cont patt to end of row. Making sure to keep patt as established, dec 1 st at armhole side every other row 2 (2, 2, 2) times. Keeping Front edge in seed st, cont until armhole is 5½ (6, 6½, 7)" [14 (15, 16.5, 18) cm], ending at Front edge.

Neck Shape

Bind off 19 (21, 24, 28,) sts st at Front edge, finish row. Making sure to keep patt as established, dec 1 st at neck edge, every other row 3 (3, 4, 4) times. Work even on rem 20 (24, 26, 28) sts until armhole is same as Back. Bind off.

Sleeves (make 2)

With size 4 needles, cast on 44 (51, 58, 58) sts. Work seed st border as for Back for 1" (2.5 cm). Change to size 6 needles. Work in patt, inc 1 st each side every 1" (2.5 cm) 13 (14, 15, 16 times) keeping inc sts in St st until there are enough sts to form a new patt. Work even on 70 (79, 88, 90) sts until Sleeve is 15½ (16, 16½, 17)" [39.5 (40.5, 42, 43) cm].

Cap Shape

Bind off 5 (5, 7, 8) sts at beg of next 2 rows. Dec 1 st each side every other row 11 (12, 13, 13) times. Bind off 2 sts at beg of next 4 (4, 6, 6) rows. Bind off rem sts.

FINISHING

Sew shoulder seams.

Neckband

With RS facing and size 4 needles, pick up 5 sts along seed st border, 19 (21, 24, 28) along bound-off edge of Right Front, 6 (7, 8, 9) sts along Right side neck shaping, 32 (38, 44, 52) sts along Back bound-off sts, 6 (7, 8, 9) sts along Left side neck shaping, 19 (21, 24, 28) sts along Left Front bound-off neck sts, 5 sts along seed st border—92 (104, 118, 136) sts. Work in seed st for 1 row, make last buttonhole on next row, cont seed st until neck border is 1" (2.5 cm). Bind off in patt.

Set in Sleeves

Mark center of sleeve cap, match center with shoulder seam, pin cap in place, easing in as you sew. Sew underarm seams. Sew on buttons.

Blocking

Lay on a padded surface, sprinkle with water, pin into shape using rust proof pins, allow to dry.

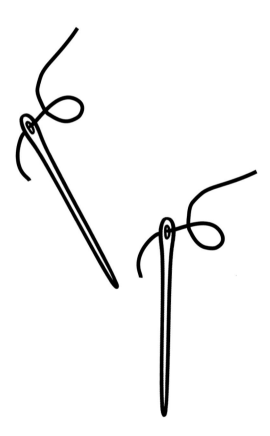

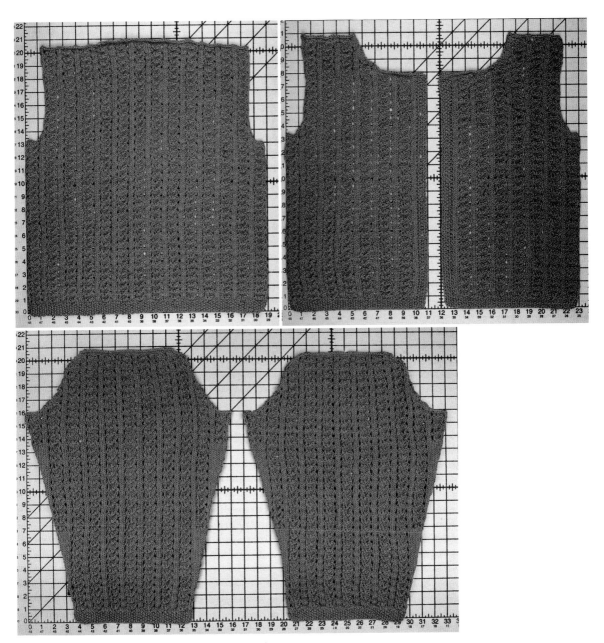

Classic Rectangle body type: pieces on blocking board

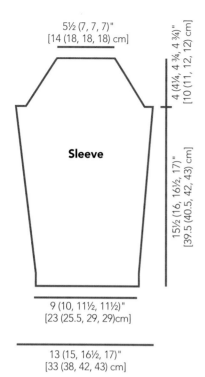

5½ (7, 7, 7)"
[14 (18, 18, 18) cm]

4 (4¼, 4 ¾, 4 ¾)"
[10 (11, 12, 12) cm]

Sleeve

15½ (16, 16½, 17)"
[39.5 (40.5, 42, 43) cm]

9 (10, 11½, 11½)"
[23 (25.5, 29, 29)cm]

13 (15, 16½, 17)"
[33 (38, 42, 43) cm]

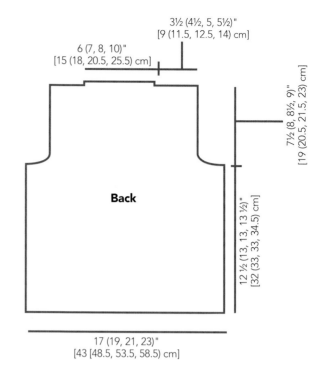

3½ (4½, 5, 5½)"
[9 (11.5, 12.5, 14) cm]

6 (7, 8, 10)"
[15 (18, 20.5, 25.5) cm]

7½ (8, 8½, 9)"
[19 (20.5, 21.5, 23) cm]

Back

12 ½ (13, 13, 13 ½)"
[32 (33, 33, 34.5) cm]

17 (19, 21, 23)"
[43 [48.5, 53.5, 58.5) cm]

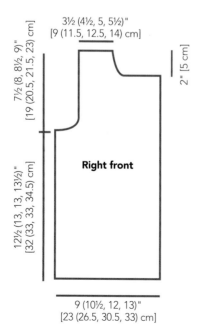

3½ (4½, 5, 5½)"
[9 (11.5, 12.5, 14) cm]

2" [5 cm]

7½ (8, 8½, 9)"
[19 (20.5, 21.5, 23) cm]

Right front

12½ (13, 13, 13½)"
[32 (33, 33, 34.5) cm]

9 (10½, 12, 13)"
[23 (26.5, 30.5, 33) cm]

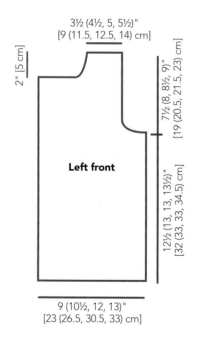

3½ (4½, 5, 5½)"
[9 (11.5, 12.5, 14) cm]

2" [5 cm]

7½ (8, 8½, 9)"
[19 (20.5, 21.5, 23) cm]

Left front

12½ (13, 13, 13½)"
[32 (33, 33, 34.5) cm]

9 (10½, 12, 13)"
[23 (26.5, 30.5, 33) cm]

Customize the Fit

INCREASING AND DECREASING THE LITTLE SHELLS PATTERN

With a pattern like Little Shells, which has a small multiple of stitches, there are a number of ways to increase stitches.

You can keep the added stitches in stockinette stitch until you have enough stiches to form a new pattern, or you can work partial patterns each time that you increase.

You can keep the added stitches in stockinette stitch (1 row knit, 1 row purl) and keep the pattern only in the center.

To decrease, eliminate a stitch from the pattern each time a decrease is made.

THE TRIANGLE BODY

If your body type is Triangle, begin your garment following a size that fits your hip measurement, then gradually decrease to fit the waist and chest measurements of a smaller size. Once you have reached your chest measurement, finish the garment following the smaller size instructions.

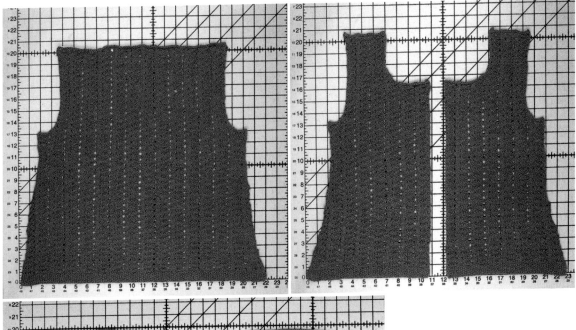

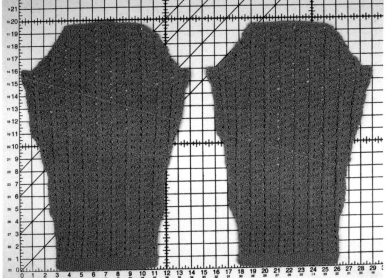

Triangle body type: pieces on blocking board

Customize the Style

To customize the style of the sweater, omit 5 seed stitches from front edges and neck. When garment is finished, add a border of Eyelet Lace (page 97) by picking up stitches at neckline first then front edges.

Instead of buttons and buttonholes, add a frog closure at waistline, made by using 2 large buttons and two EZ Cords (page 107).

THE INVERTED TRIANGLE

If your body type is Inverted Triangle, begin your garment following a size that fits your hip measurement, then gradually increase to the waist and chest measurement of a larger size. Once you have reached your chest measurement, finish the garment following the larger size instructions.

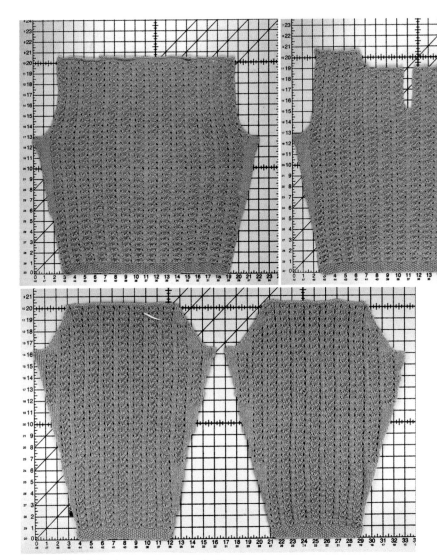

Inverted Triangle body type: pieces on blocking board

Customize the Style

To customize the style of this sweater, I turned it into a pullover. For Front, follow the instructions as for the Back of the sweater until after armhole shaping is completed. At this point, divide work in half, work each side separately and shape as neckline for Classic Cardigan. For neck border, pick up and work seed stitch for 5 rows, working a two row buttonhole (page 88) on the second and third row of top Right Front. No finishing is necessary on the placket edges.

THE HOURGLASS

If your body type is Hourglass, begin your garment following a size that fits your hip measurement, then gradually decrease to your waist measurement, work about 2 inches (5 centimeters) even, then gradually increase to your chest measurement. Once you have reached your chest measurement, finish the garment following the size that fits your chest measurement.

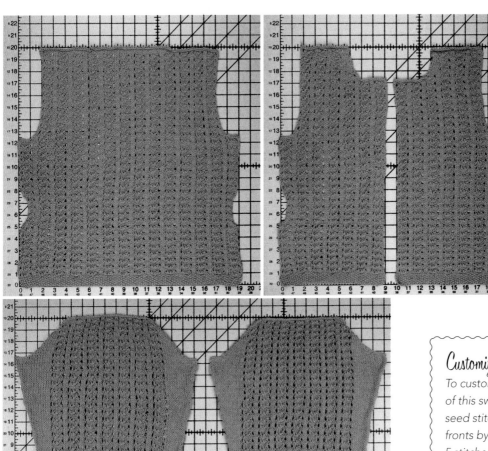

Hourglass body type: pieces on blocking board

Customize the Style

To customize the style of this sweater, omit the seed stitch border on fronts by casting on 5 stitches less than the instructions call for in the classic cardigan. When sweater is finished, work the seed stitch neck border. For Front bands, work two Vertical Eyelet Lace edgings (page 103) to fit front edges when slightly stretched, pin, sew in place. No need to make buttonholes as this trim makes evenly spaced little holes. Sew buttons evenly spaced on Left Front, use corresponding holes for buttonholes.

Traveling Vines Pullover

There are many open, lacy knit pattern stitches that require a large multiple plus the use of many yarn-overs to complete the pattern. Traveling Vines is one of these patterns. The large multiple plus the use of many yarn-overs makes customizing the fit of these garment patterns quite difficult. I find that changing the needle size, rather than increasing or decreasing stitches, works quite well and is much easier to manage.

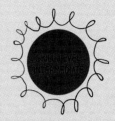

CLASSIC RECTANGLE

Yarn: Light ❸

Shown: LB Collection Superwash Merino, 100% Superwash Merino Wool, 3.5 oz (100 g)/306 yds (280 m): Peony, 5 (5, 6, 7) skeins

Needles: Sizes 4 (3.5 mm) and 6 (4 mm) or size needed to obtain gauge

Take time to check gauge.

Gauge: 3 patt repeats = 4" (10 cm) on size 6 needles

Take time to check gauge.

Notions:

Stitch holders

Tapestry needle

Sizes: Small (Medium, Large, X-Large)

Finished chest: 34 (38, 42, 46)" [86.5 (96.5, 106.5, 117) cm]

Finished length: 20 (21, 21½, 22 ½)" [51 (53.5, 54.5, 57) cm]

Notes: Pattern is multiple of 8 plus 2. If through back loop (tbl) is stated, knit or purl through the back loop of the stitch; however if through back loop is not stated, knit or purl in usual manner.

All slip stitches are slipped pwise.

BACK

With size 6 needles, cast on 90 (106, 122, 138) sts. Work patt as follows:

Row 1: K1, *yo, k1 tbl, yo skp, k5, rep from * to last st, k1.

Row 2: K1, *p4, p2tog tbl, p3, rep from * across to last st, k1.

Row 3: K1, *yo, k1 tbl, yo, k2, skp, k3, rep from * to last st, k1.

Row 4: K1, *p2, p2tog tbl, p5, rep from * to last st, k1.

Row 5: K1, *k1 tbl, yo, k4, skp, k1, yo, rep from * to last st, k1.

Row 6: K1, *p1, p2tog tbl, p6, rep from * to last st, k1.

Row 7: K1, *k5, k2tog, yo, k1 tbl, yo, rep from * to last st, k1.

Row 8: K1, *p3, p2tog, p4, rep from * to last st, k1.

Row 9: K1, *k3, k2tog, k2, yo, k1 tbl, yo, rep from * to last st, k1.

Row 10: K1, *p5, p2tog, p2, rep from * to last st, k1.

Row 11: K1, *yo, k1, k2tog, k4, yo, k1 tbl, rep from * to last st, k1.

Row 12: K1, *p6, p2tog, p1, rep from * to last st, k1.

Rep Rows 1–12 until piece measures 12½ (13, 13, 13½)" [32 (33, 33, 34.5) cm] from beg.

Armhole Shape

Bind off 8 (8, 8, 8) sts at beg of next 2 rows. Making sure to keep patt as established, cont even in patt on 74 (90, 106, 122) sts until armhole is 7½ (8, 8½, 9)" [19 (20.5, 21.5, 23) cm].

Shoulder Shape

Bind off 18 (24, 26, 28) sts at beg of next 2 rows. Place rem 38 (42, 54, 66) sts on holder to be worked later for neckband.

FRONT

Work same as Back until armhole measures 5 (5½, 6, 6½)" [12.5 (14, 15, 16.5) cm], ending with a WS row.

Shape Neck

Next Row (RS): Work across 18 (24, 26, 28) for left neck, turn. Work on these sts only, making sure to keep patt as established, until armhole measures same as Back. Bind off.

With RS facing, place center 38 (42, 54, 66) sts on holder for center neck, join yarn and work rem 18 (24, 26, 28) sts for right neck until piece measures same as Back. Bind off.

SLEEVES (MAKE TWO)

With size 4 needles, cast on 50 (58, 66, 74) sts. Work patt same as Back for 2" (5 cm).

Change to size 6 needles and cont in patt, inc 1 st each side every 1" (2.5 cm) 12 (12, 12, 12) times), keeping inc sts in St st. Work even for 74 (82, 90, 98) sts until sleeve is 17½ (18, 18 ½, 19)" [44.4 (45.5, 47, 49.5) cm]. Bind off loosely. (It is very important that this bind off is done loosely; if necessary, use a larger needle to bind off.)

FINISHING

Sew left shoulder. With RS facing, using size 4 needles, join yarn at right Back neck, k38 (42, 54, 66) sts from Back neck holder, pick up and k7 (8, 9, 10) sts along left neck edge, k38 (42, 54, 66) sts from Front holder, pick up and k7 (8, 9, 10) sts along right neck edge—90 (100, 126, 152) sts. Work in St st (purl 1 row, knit 1 row) for 11 rows Using size 6 needles, bind off loosely in knit.

Sew right shoulder seam and edges of neckband. Allow neckband to roll naturally to Front.

Sew in sleeves: Fold Sleeve in half, mark the center, pin in place with center of Sleeve at shoulder seam and end of bound off edge of Sleeve at inner edge of bound-off underarm sts, then sew in place. Sew underarm seams. Weave in ends.

EMBELLISHMENT

Make one Knit Flower 2 (page 105) and two Small Leaves (page 105).

Blocking: Place garment on a padded surface, sprinkle with water, pat into shape, pinning points of patt using rust-proof pins. Repeat for the embellishments. Allow to dry.

Sew the leaves and flower to the left front shoulder.

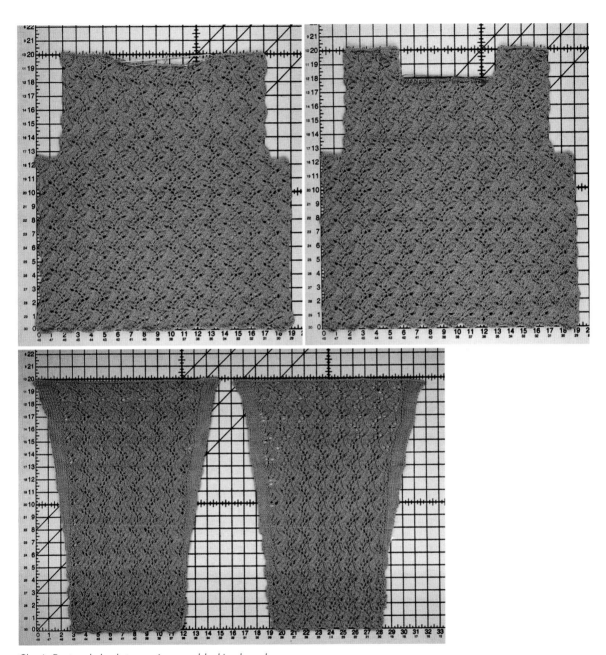

Classic Rectangle body type: pieces on blocking board

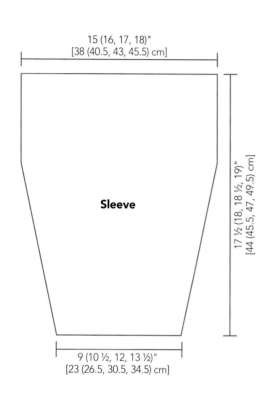

15 (16, 17, 18)"
[38 (40.5, 43, 45.5) cm]

Sleeve

17 ½ (18, 18 ½, 19)"
[44 (45.5, 47, 49.5) cm]

9 (10 ½, 12, 13 ½)"
[23 (26.5, 30.5, 34.5) cm]

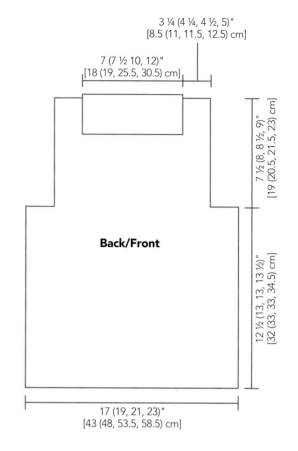

3 ¼ (4 ¼, 4 ½, 5)"
[8.5 (11, 11.5, 12.5) cm]

7 (7 ½ 10, 12)"
[18 (19, 25.5, 30.5) cm]

Back/Front

7 ½ (8, 8 ½, 9)"
[19 (20.5, 21.5, 23) cm]

12 ½ (13, 13, 13 ½)"
[32 (33, 33, 34.5) cm]

17 (19, 21, 23)"
[43 (48, 53.5, 58.5) cm]

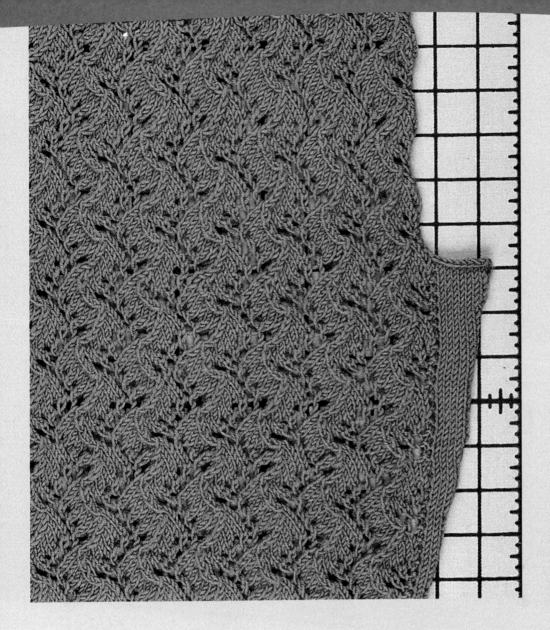

Customize the Fit

Traveling Vines is a difficult pattern to increase and decrease and still keep the pattern going, so it is advisable to keep any added stitches in Stockinette Stitch.

When decreasing and increasing, such as in the hour glass shape, use larger and smaller needles to decrease and keep the pattern stitches the same.

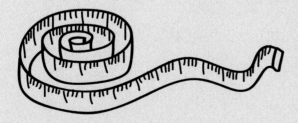

THE TRIANGLE BODY

If your body type is Triangle, begin your garment following a size that fits your hip measurement, then gradually decrease to fit the waist and chest measurements of a smaller size. Once you have reached your chest measurement, finish the garment following the smaller size instructions.

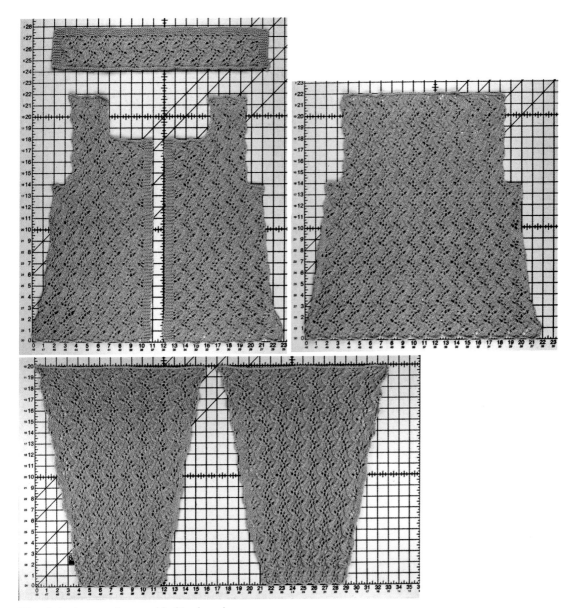

Triangle body type: pieces on blocking board

Customize the Style

A pullover style can be changed to a cardigan.

FRONTS

Divide the Front of Pullover in half (when turning a pullover into a cardigan by dividing the Front in half, be sure to take into consideration the multiple of the stitch pattern. If only a few stitches are needed, they may be kept in stockinette stitch or reverse stockinette stitch) add 5 stitches to each Front, to accommodate a garter stitch border. Continue working in pattern, shaping arm sides as back. When armhole is 5 (5.5, 6, 6.5)" [12.5 (14, 15, 16.5) cm] bind off neck edge leaving 16, (24, 26, 28) sts at arm side.

Continue working on these stitches until same as back to shoulder.

Collar: Using the #6 needle, cast on the same amount of stitches as back of garment plus 10 more stitches. Work garter stitch for 1" (2.5 cm), continue to work pattern as for back, keeping 5 stitches each side in garter stitch, for 4"(10 cm), bind off.

EMBELLISHMENTS

Using the #6 needle, make 4 small leaf motifs page 105.

Small Leaf ties (Make 2): work a 3 stitch I-Cord (page 107) for 8" (20.5 cm), increase 1 st each side (5 sts) continue to work a small leaf motif at end of cord.

Assembly: After Garment is sewn together, mark center of collar, and center back of neck. Pin right Side of collar to wrong side of garment, matching center and having ends of collar at very end of seed stitch border, sew collar in place. Turn top edges of Front and Collar to right side of sweater and tack down. Arrange the Small Leaf Ties and remaining Leaves as in photo.

THE INVERTED TRIANGLE

If your body type is Inverted Triangle, begin your garment following a size that fits your hip measurement, then gradually increase to the waist and chest measurement of a larger size. Once you have reached your chest measurement, finish the garment following the larger size instructions.

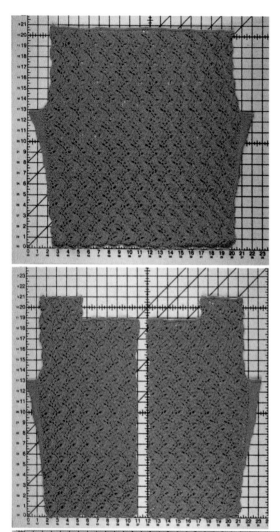

Detail of increases under arm

Inverted triangle body type: pieces on blocking board

Customize the Style

To customize the style of this sweater, divide the Front of Pullover in half (when turning a pullover into a cardigan by dividing the Front in half, be sure to take into consideration the multiple of the stitch pattern) it may be necessary to add a few stitches. Continue working in pattern, shaping arm sides back. When armhole is 5 (5.5, 6, 6.5)" [12.5 (14, 15,16.5) cm] bind off neck edge leaving 16, (24, 26, 28) sts at arm side.

Continue working on these stitches until same as back to shoulder, bind off.

FRONT BORDERS

Left Front: When garment is all sewn together, using the #4 needle, with right side facing you, pick up stitches along Left Front edge, work garter stitch (knit every row) for 5 rows, bind off.

Right Front: Before starting Right Front, place markers on Left front border for 5 button placements, having bottom button about 4" (10 cm) from bottom, top button ½" (1.3 cm) from top.

Soft ruffle at neckline

Row 1 and 2: Knit.

Row 3 (Buttonhole Row): Knit, working first part of Two-Row Buttonhole (page 88) using markers as guide for placement.

Row 4: Knit, working second part of Two-Row Buttonhole.

Row 5: Knit.

Bind off.

RUFFLE NECK

Row 1: Using # 6 needle, with right side facing you, start at beginning of pattern on Right Front, and leaving Right Border free, pick up stitches from bound-off edge, side of neck, back, Left side neck edges, and Left bound-off stitches, leaving Left Border free.

Row 1: Purl.

Row 2: Knit.

Row 3: * K3, inc 1 st in next st, rep from * to end.

Row 4: *K2, inc 1 st in next st, rep from * to end.

Row 5: K1, inc 1 st in next st, rep from * to end.

Row 6: Knit.

Row 7: Bind off in knit.

THE HOURGLASS

If your body type is Hourglass, begin your garment following a size that fits your hip measurement, then gradually decrease to your waist measurement, work about 2" (5 cm) even, then gradually increase to your chest measurement. Once you have reached your chest measurement, finish the garment following the size that fits your chest measurement. Because this stitch is a little tricky to increase and decrease, for the Hourglass shape, we used needle sizes to create the shaping. Instead of the usual increasing and decreasing, we changed needle size from 6 to 4 for the 2" (5 cm) at waistline, then went back to size 6 needle, then 7 to achieve chest measurement. We also shaped the sleeve by starting with #4 needles for 12 rows, #5 needles for 36 rows, #6 needles for 36 rows, #7 needles to finish. This is just an alternative method of increasing and decreasing; the conventional method may be used for any garment.

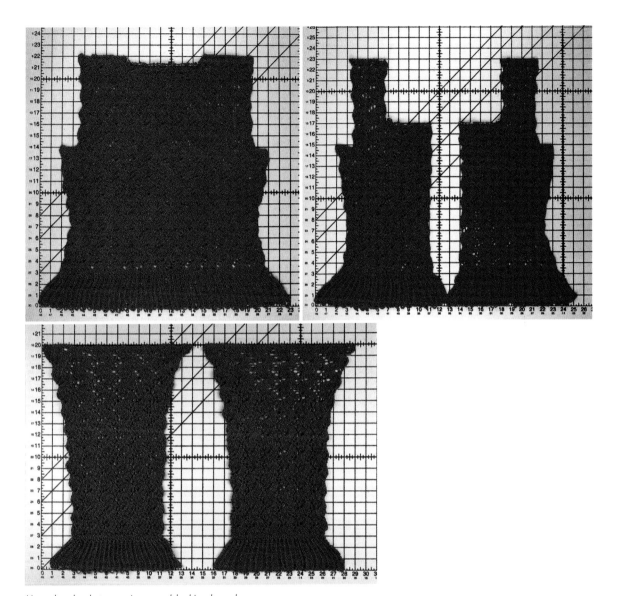

Hourglass body type: pieces on blocking board

Customize the Style

Drop Stitch Edging forms a gentle, lacy ruffle

To customize the style of this sweater, divide the Front of Pullover in half (when turning a pullover into a cardigan by dividing the Front in half, be sure to take into consideration the multiple of the stitch pattern) it may be necessary to add a few stitches. We also added the Drop Stitch Edging (page 99), which requires some figuring. It is important to remember that one third of the stitches will be dropped, so add one third more stitches to your cast on number. Continue working, in pattern, shaping arm sides as back. When armhole is 3 (3½, 4, 4½)" [7.5 (9,10,11.5) cm], bind off neck edge leaving 16, (24, 26, 28) sts at arm side.

Continue working on these stitches until same as back to shoulder, bind off.

When garment is sewn together, using #4 needles, right side facing you, pick up stitches around neckline, work k1, p1 in ribbing for 1" (2.5 cm), bind off in ribbing.

Front Border: This border is done in single crochet, using a #5 crochet hook. See page 83 for Crochet Borders. If you do prefer, any knit border from one of the other cardigans may be substituted.

LEFT FRONT

Row 1 and 3: Starting at top Left Front, work 1 row sc down to end of Drop Stich Edging , ch 1, turn.

Row 2 and 4: One sc in each sc to top, ch 1, turn.

Row 5: 1 sc in each sc to end of row, ch 1, do not turn.

Row 6: Work 1 row reverse sc to end of row.

Right Front: Before starting Right Front, mark Left Front for 6 buttonholes, placing top buttonhole about ½" (1.3 cm) from top and bottom buttonhole about 3½" (9 cm) from bottom.

Row 1: Starting at bottom of Right Front, work 1 row sc up to top of Ribbed border, ch 1, turn.

Row 2: One sc in each sc to end of row, ch 1, turn.

Row 3: Begin Buttonholes, work sc to first marker, ch 2, sk 2, *work sc to next marker, ch 2, sk 2, rep from * until 6 buttonholes are made, sc to end of row, ch 1 turn.

Row 4: Complete Buttonholes, work sc to first ch-2 space, work 2 sc in space, *sc to next ch-2 sp, 2 sc in ch-2 space, rep from * to last ch-2 sp, sc to end of row, ch 1 turn.

Row 5: 1 sc in each sc, ch 1, do not turn.

Row 6: Work 1 row reverse sc to end of row, fasten off.

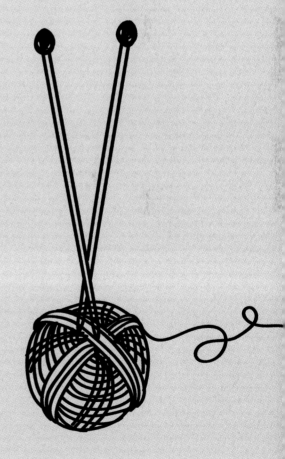

Pineapple Twist Cardigan

Pineapple Twist is a pattern that will test your knitting skills. While not the easiest of stitch patterns, it does produce a very impressive fabric, and when you finish this cardigan, your friends will be asking "did you really make that?" This pattern can be shaped in a few different ways, by increasing and decreasing stitches at the ends, or by increasing or decreasing the number of stitches between the twists.

SKILL LEVEL
EXPERIENCED

CLASSIC RECTANGLE

Yarn: LB Collection Superwash Merino, 100% Superwash Merino Wool, 306 yds/280m, 3.5oz/100g, 5 (6, 6, 7) skeins Spring Green

Needles: Sizes 4 (3.5 mm) and 6 (4 mm) or size needed to obtain gauge

Gauge: 27 sts = 4" (10 cm) in cable patt on size 6 needles

3 patt repeats of 11 sts = 4" (10 cm) on size 6 needles

34 rows = 4" (10 cm)

Take time to check gauge.

Notions:

Small cable needle

Six ⅝" (1.6 cm) buttons

Stitch markers

Tapestry needle

Sizes: Small (Medium, Large, X-Large)

Finished chest: 34 (38, 42, 46)" [86.5 (96.5, 106.5, 117) cm]

Finished length: 20 ½ (21 ½, 22 ½, 23 ½)" [52 (54.5, 57, 59.5) cm]

BACK

With size 4 needles, cast on 115 (125, 135, 145) sts. Work k1, p1 ribbing for 1½" (4 cm).

Purl one row, inc 10 sts evenly across row—125 (135, 145, 155) sts.

Change to size 6 needles and work as follows:

Note: *Pattern is worked between markers on M, L, XL; stitches on sides are worked in stockinette stitch.*

Row 1 (RS): K0 (5, 10, 15), place marker, *p4, seed st on next 7 sts**, p4, k7; rep from * across, ending last rep at **, p4, place marker, k0 (5, 10, 15).

Row 2: P0 (5, 10, 15), *k4, seed st on 7 sts, k4**, p7; rep from * across, ending last rep at **, p0 (5, 10, 15).

Row 3: Same as Row 1.

Row 4: Same as Row 2.

Row 5 (first twist row): K0 (5, 10, 15), *p4, seed st on next 7 sts**, p4, slip next 4 sts to cable needle, hold to front of work, k next 3 sts, k4 sts from cable needle; rep from * across ending last rep at **, p4, k0 (5, 10, 15).

Row 6: Same as Row 2.

Row 7: Same as Row 1.

Row 8: Same as Row 2.

Row 9: Same as Row 1.

Row 10: Same as Row 2.

Row 11 (second twist row): Same as Row 5.

Row 12: Same as Row 2.

Row 13 (change row): K0 (5, 10, 15), *p4, k7, p4**, seed st on next 7 sts; rep from * across ending last rep at **, k0 (5, 10, 15).

Row 14: P0 (5, 10, 15), *k4, p7, k4**, seed on next 7 sts; rep from * across, ending last rep at **, p0 (5, 10, 15).

Row 15: K0 (5, 10, 15), *p4, k7, p4**, seed st on next 7 sts; rep from * across, ending last rep at **, k0 (5, 10, 15).

Row 16: Same as Row 14.

Row 17 (twist row): K0 (5, 10, 15), *p4, slip next 4 sts to cable needle, hold to front of work, k3, k4 from cable needle, p4**, seed on next 7 sts; rep from * across, ending last rep at **, k0, (5, 10, 15).

Row 18: Same as Row 14.

Row 19: Same as Row 15.

Row 20: Same as Row 14.

Row 21: Same as Row 15.

Row 22: Same as Row 14.

Row 23 (twist row): Same as Row 17.

Row 24: P0 (5, 10, 15), *k4, p7, k4**, seed st on next 7 sts, k4; rep from * across, ending last rep at **, p0 (5, 10, 15).

Rep Rows 1–24 for patt until 13 (13 ½, 14, 14 ½)" [33 (34.5, 35.5, 37) cm] from beg.

Armhole Shape

Making sure to keep patt as est, bind off 5 (6, 7, 8) sts at beg of next 2 rows—115 (123, 131,139) sts. Cont in patt, dec 1 st each side every other row 2 (2, 2, 2) times—111 (119, 127, 135) sts. Work even until armhole is 7 ½ (8, 8 ½, 9)" [19 (20.5, 21.5, 23) cm].

Shoulder Shape

Bind off 32 (34, 36, 38) sts at beg of next 2 rows. Bind off rem 47 (51, 55, 59) sts.

LEFT FRONT

With size 4 needles, cast on 58 (63, 68, 73) sts.

Row 1: K1, p1 in ribbing until last 5 sts, place marker, seed st on last 5 sts (Front border).

Row 2: Seed st on first 5 sts, ribbing to end.

Rep Rows 1 and 2 for 1½" (4 cm), ending at Front edge.

Next row: Seed st on first 5 sts, purl rem sts, inc 6 sts evenly spaced—64 (69, 74, 79) sts.

Change to size 6 needles, work as follows:

Row 1: K0 (5, 10, 15) place marker, work patt Row 1 until last 5 sts, seed st on last 5 sts.

Row 2: Seed st on first 5 sts, patt Row 2 until last 0 (5, 10, 15) sts, purl rem sts.

Cont in this manner, keeping 5 sts at Front edge in seed st and sts between markers in patt same as Back until armhole is same as Back, ending at arm edge.

Armhole Shape

Bind off 5 (6, 7, 8) sts at beg of next row, then cont patt to end of row.

Making sure to keep patt as established, dec 1 st at arm side every other row 2 (2, 2, 2) times. Work even on rem 57 (61, 65, 69) sts until armhole is 5 ½ (6, 6 ½, 7)" [14 (15, 16.5, 18) cm], ending at Front edge.

Neck Shape

Bind off 18 (20, 22, 24) sts at beg of next row, then cont patt to end of row. Making sure to keep patt as established, cont to dec 1 st at neck edge, every other row 7 times. Work even on rem 32 (34, 36, 38) sts until armhole measures same as Back. Bind off rem sts.

RIGHT FRONT

Before beginning Right Front, mark Left Front for six buttonholes evenly spaced, starting at center of bottom border and allowing for top buttonhole to be worked in center of Neck border. As you work the seed st border, work a two-row buttonhole as shown on page 88 by each marked place on Left Front.

With size 4 needles, cast on 58 (63, 68, 73) sts,

Row 1: Seed st on first 5 sts, (Front button band), place marker, K1, p1 ribbing to end of row.

Row 2: K1, p1 ribbing to last 5 sts, seed st on 5 sts.

Rep Rows 1 and 2 for 1 ½" (4 cm), ending at arm side.

Next Row: Purl across first 53 (58, 63, 68) sts inc 6 sts evenly spaced, then work seed st, on last 5 sts—64 (69, 74, 79) sts.

Change to size 6 needles work as follows:

Row 1: Seed st on first 5 sts, work patt Row 1 until last 0 (5, 10, 15) sts, k rem sts.

Row 2: P0 (5, 10, 15), patt to last 5 sts, seed on last 5 sts.

Cont in this manner, keeping 5 sts at Front edge in seed st and sts between markers in patt same as Back until armhole is same as Back, ending at arm edge.

Armhole Shape

Bind off 5 (6, 7, 8) sts at beg of next row, then cont patt to end of row.

Making sure to keep patt as est, dec 1 st at arm side every other row 2 (2, 2, 2) times. Work even on rem 57 (61, 65, 69) sts until armhole is 5 ½ (6, 6 ½, 7)" [14 (15, 16.5, 18) cm], ending at Front edge.

Neck Shape

Bind off 18 (20, 22, 24) sts at beg of next row, then cont patt to end of row. Making sure to keep patt as est, cont to dec 1 st at neck edge, every other row 7 times. Work even on rem 32 (34, 36, 38) sts until armhole measures same as Back. Bind off rem sts.

SLEEVES (MAKE 2)

Cast on 58 (60, 62, 64) sts. Work K1, p1 ribbing for 1 ½" (4 cm). Purl one row, inc to 59 (63, 67, 71) sts. Work as follows:

Row 1 (RS):, K0 (2, 4, 6), place marker on needle, *p4, seed st on next 7 sts**, p4, k7; rep from * ending last rep at **, p4, place marker, k0 (2, 4, 6).

Row 2: P0 (2, 4, 6), *k4, seed st on 7 sts, k4**, p7; rep from * end last rep at **, p0 (2, 4, 6).

Cont in this manner, working patt rows as on Back, and at the same time, inc 1 st each side at 1" (2.5 cm) above border and every 1 ½" (4 cm) thereafter, keeping added sts in stockinette st, 10 times—79 (83, 87, 91) sts.

Work even in patt as established until Sleeve measures 16 (16, 16 ½, 16 ½)" [40.5 (40.5, 42, 42) cm] from beg.

Cap Shape

Bind off 5 (6, 7, 8) sts at beg of next 2 rows. Cont in patt, dec 1 st each side every other row 12 (13, 14, 15) times—45 (45, 45, 45 sts). Bind off 2 sts at beg of next 4 rows. Bind off rem 37 (37, 37, 37) sts.

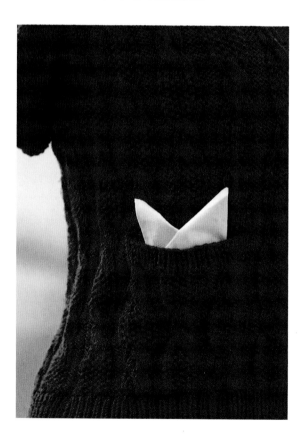

POCKETS (MAKE 2)

With size 6 needles, cast on 33 sts.

Row 1 (RS): P2, place marker, work patt Row 1 until last 2 sts, p2.

Row 2: K2, patt Row 2 until last 2 sts, k2.

Cont in this manner, keeping 2 sts at each edge in reverse stockinette st and 29 sts between markers in patt until piece measures 4 ¼" (11 cm).

Change to size 4 needles. Work in K1, p1 ribbing for ¾" (2 cm). Bind off.

FINISHING

Sew shoulder seams.

Neckband

With RS facing you and a size 4 needle, starting at top Right Front, pick up 18 (20, 22, 24) sts along bound-off edge, 16 (16, 16, 16) sts along side of neck, 47 (51, 55, 59) along Back bind off, 16 (16, 16, 16) sts along side of neck, 18 (20, 22, 24) sts along top of Left Front—115 (123, 131, 139) sts. Work in ribbing for 1" (2.5 cm), Bind off in patt.

Set in Sleeves: Mark center of Sleeve cap and match center of Sleeve cap to shoulder seam. Match armhole bound-off sts on Sleeve and body, pin, easing into shape, then sew in Sleeve cap. Sew underarm Sleeve and body seams.

Sew pockets in place. Sew on buttons opposite button holes.

Blocking: Lay garment on a padded surface, sprinkle with water and lightly pat into shape, pin if necessary. Pressing this pattern with a steam iron is not recommended.

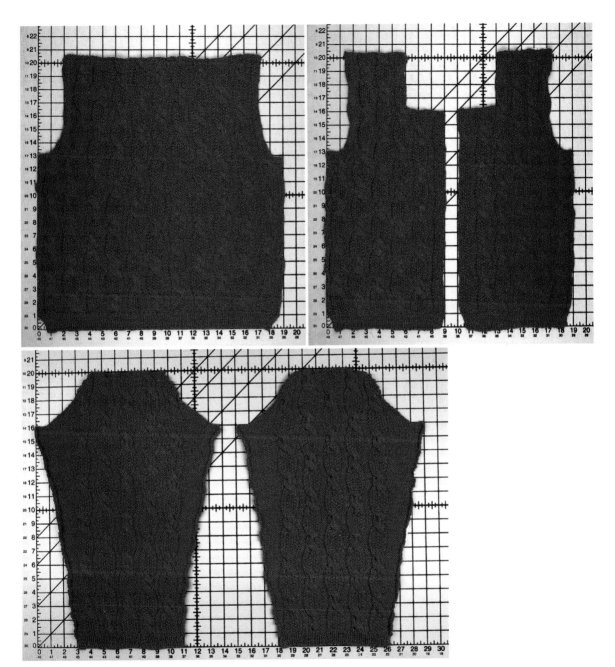

Classic Rectangle body type: pieces on blocking board

Customize the Fit

When increasing this pattern, it is best to keep the added stitches in Stockinette Stitch (1 row knit, 1 row purl) but use the purl side as the right side of work, as it fits in better with the pattern.

When decreasing this pattern, keep pattern as established, eliminating one stitch each time a decrease is made.

THE TRIANGLE

If your body type is Triangle, begin your garment following a size that fits your hip measurement, then gradually decrease to fit the waist and chest measurements of a smaller size. Once you have reached your chest measurement, finish the garment following the smaller size instructions.

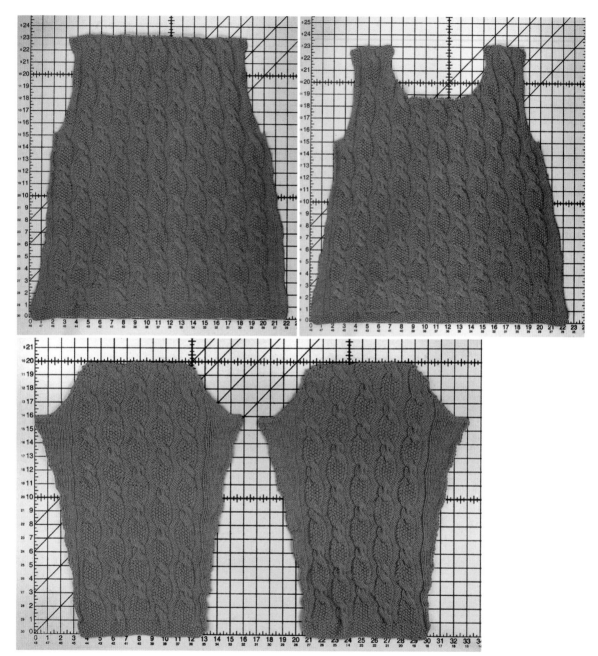

Triangle body type: pieces on blocking board

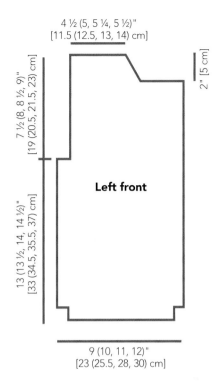

4 ½ (5, 5 ¼, 5 ½)"
[11.5 (12.5, 13, 14) cm]

2" [5 cm]

7 ½ (8, 8 ½, 9)"
[19 (20.5, 21.5, 23) cm]

Left front

13 (13 ½, 14, 14 ½)"
[33 (34.5, 35.5, 37) cm]

9 (10, 11, 12)"
[23 (25.5, 28, 30) cm]

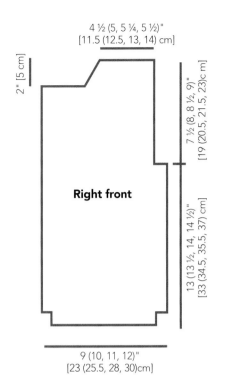

4 ½ (5, 5 ¼, 5 ½)"
[11.5 (12.5, 13, 14) cm]

2" [5 cm]

7 ½ (8, 8 ½, 9)"
[19 (20.5, 21.5, 23)c m]

Right front

13 (13 ½, 14, 14 ½)"
[33 (34.5, 35.5, 37) cm]

9 (10, 11, 12)"
[23 (25.5, 28, 30)cm]

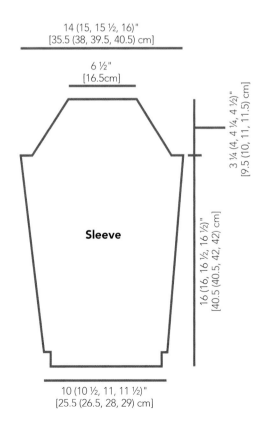

14 (15, 15 ½, 16)"
[35.5 (38, 39.5, 40.5) cm]

6 ½"
[16.5cm]

3 ¼ (4, 4 ¼, 4 ½)"
[9.5 (10, 11, 11.5) cm]

Sleeve

16 (16, 16 ½, 16 ½)"
[40.5 (40.5, 42, 42) cm]

10 (10 ½, 11, 11 ½)"
[25.5 (26.5, 28, 29) cm]

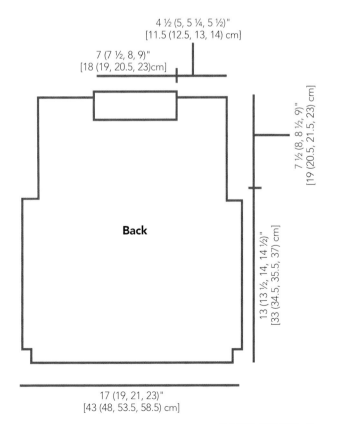

4 ½ (5, 5 ¼, 5 ½)"
[11.5 (12.5, 13, 14) cm]

7 (7 ½, 8, 9)"
[18 (19, 20.5, 23)cm]

7 ½ (8, 8 ½, 9)"
[19 (20.5, 21.5, 23) cm]

Back

13 (13 ½, 14, 14 ½)"
[33 (34.5, 35.5, 37) cm]

17 (19, 21, 23)"
[43 (48, 53.5, 58.5) cm]

Customize the Style

Pullover with turtle neck

To customize the style of this sweater, we turned it into a pullover with a cozy turtleneck and added a seed stitch border to bottom instead of ribbing. Begin by following the Back instructions, until shoulder measurement is reached. Shape Shoulder and Neck as follows: at the beginning of the next 2 rows bind off 22 (24, 26, 28) sts, bind off remaining 67 (71, 75, 79) sts.

Work Front same as back until armhole is 3" (7.5 cm) shorter than Back. Shape neck as follows: Making sure to keep pattern as established, work across 37 (39, 41, 43) sts, join a new ball of yarn, bind off center 37 (41, 45, 49), work remaining 37 (39, 41, 43) sts. Working each side with separate balls of yarn, and making sure to keep pattern as established, decrease one stitch at neck edges, every row 15 times. Work even on remaining 22, (24, 26, 28) sts until same as Back to shoulder, bind off.

You will need circular needles #4 and #6 to add the turtleneck. Using the #4 circular needle, starting at right shoulder, right side facing you, pick up 67 (71, 75, 79) stitches along back of neck, 15 (15, 15, 15) along side of Left Front, 37 (41, 45, 49) center Front, 15 (15, 15, 15) along right side of neck 138 (142, 150, 158) sts. Working in the round, k1, p1 in ribbing for 3" (7.5 cm), change to the #6 needle, continue ribbing for 3" (7.5 cm) more, bind off loosely in ribbing.

THE INVERTED TRIANGLE

If your body type is Inverted Triangle, begin your garment following a size that fits your hip measurement, then gradually increase to the waist and chest measurement of a larger size. Once you have reached your chest measurement, finish the garment following the larger size instructions.

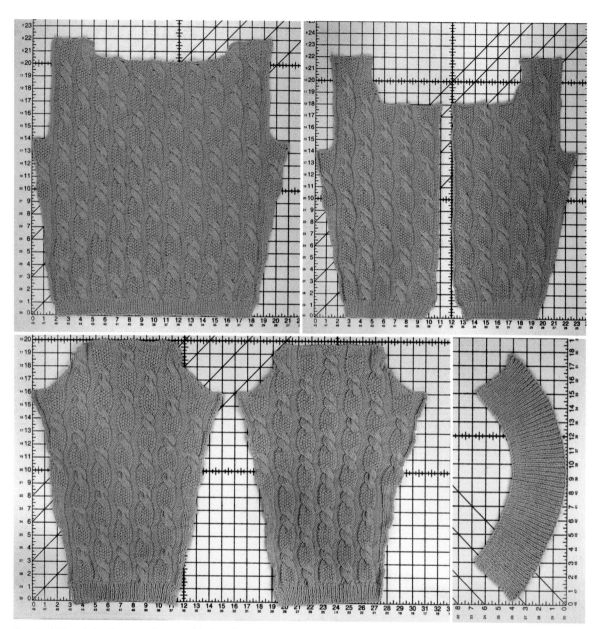

Inverted Triangle body type: pieces on blocking board

Customize the Style

Left open, this style balances narrow hips and wide shoulders.

To customize the style of this sweater, omit 5 seed stitches for the Front Border. Make 2 Large Garter Stitch Scallop Borders (page 103) as follows:

For Left Front: With #6 needles make a border to fit front edge from bottom to top when slightly stretched. Mark scallops for 5 evenly spaced buttons.

For Right Front: Work as for Left Front, using the markers as a guide, make a two-row buttonhole (page 88) in rows 8 and 9 of marked scallops. Sew Borders to Fronts of sweater.

Collar: Using #4 needles, cast on 126 (130, 134, 138) sts, k1, p1 in ribbing for 1" (2.5 cm), change to the #6 needles, continue ribbing until collar is 4 (4, 4½, 4½)" [10, (10, 11.5, 11.5) cm] bind off loosely in ribbing.

Mark center of collar and center of back neck, pin collar in place, matching centers and having ends of collar inside Front borders, sew in place.

Sew on buttons.

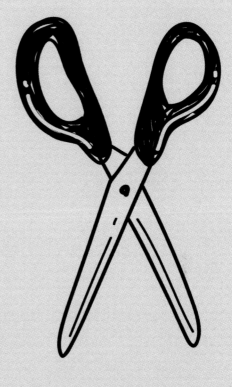

THE HOURGLASS

If your body type is Hourglass, begin your garment following a size that fits your hip measurement, then gradually decrease to your waist measurement, work about 2" (5 cm) even, then gradually increase to your chest measurement. Once you have reached your chest measurement, finish the garment following the size that fits your chest measurement.

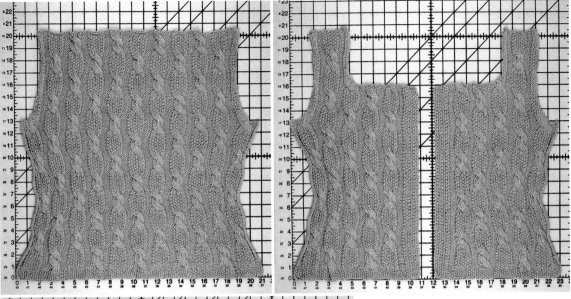

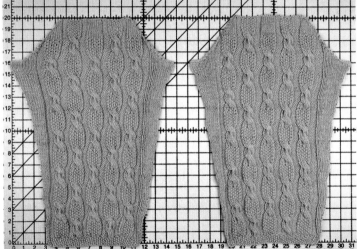

Hourglass body type: pieces on blocking board

Customize the Style

To customize the style of this sweater, use seed stitch for all the borders instead of ribbing and omit buttonholes. Add 3 buttonhole tabs on right Front as follows: Starting at edge of Right Front neck border, pick up 7 sts, work in seed stitch for 3 rows, on the 4th and 5th row, work a two-row buttonhole, seed st on rows 6, 7, and 8, bind off. Add two more buttonhole tabs spaced about 3" (7.5 cm) apart.

Climbing Leaf Hoodie

The Climbing Leaf pattern is for the experienced knitter. The pattern does have quite a few rows and a large multiple, but once the pattern is established and you see it emerge, it becomes easier. The best way to customize this pattern is by increasing or decreasing the sides and keeping the extra stitches in Stockinette Stitch or Reverse Stockinette Stitch.

SKILL LEVEL
EXPERIENCED

CLASSIC RECTANGLE

Yarn: Light (3)

Shown: LB Collection Superwash Merino, 100% Superwash Merino Wool, 306 yds/280m, 3.5oz/100g, 7 (7, 8, 8) skeins Wisteria

Needles: Sizes 4 (3.5 mm) and 6 (4 mm) straight needles or size needed to obtain gauge

Size 4 (3.5 mm) circular needle for border

Gauge: 1 patt repeat = 5" (12.5 cm) on size 6 needles

34 rows = 4" (10 cm) on size 6 needles

Take time to check gauge.

Notions: Tapestry needle

One 20 (20, 22, 22)" [51 (51, 56, 56) cm] separating zipper

Note: *Zippers come in 2" (5 cm) increments, so adjust sweater Front length measurement to accommodate zipper.*

Sizes: Small (Medium, Large, X-Large)

Finished chest: 36 (40, 44, 48)" [91.5 (101.5, 112, 122) cm]

Finished length: 21 (22, 23, 24)" [53.5 (56, 58.5, 61) cm]

Climbing Leaf Stitch Pattern

Worked on 29 stitches.

Row 1: K3, p2, k4, k2tog, k3, yo, k1, yo, k3, sl 1, k1, psso (skp), k4, p2, k3.

Row 2: K5, p5, k3, p3, k3, p5, k5.

Row 3: K3, p2, k3, k2tog, k4, yo, k1, yo, k4, skp, k3, p2, k3.

Row 4: K5, p4, k3, p5, k3, p4, k5.

Row 5: K3, p2, k2, k2tog, k5, yo, k1, yo, k5, skp, k2, p2, k3.

Row 6: K5, p3, k3, p7, k3, p3, k5.

Row 7: K3, p2, k1, k2tog, k6, yo, k1, yo, k6, skp, k1, p2, k3.

Row 8: K5, p2, k3, p9, k3, p2, k5.

Row 9: K3, p2, k2tog, k7, yo, k1, yo, k7, skp, p2, k3.

Row 10: K5, p1, k3, p11, k3, p1, k5.

Row 11: K3, p2, k1, yo, k3, skp, k7, k2tog, k3, yo, k1, p2, k3.

Row 12: K5, p2, k3, p9, k3, p2, k5.

Row 13: K3, p2, k2, yo, k3, skp, k5, k2tog, k3, yo, k2, p2, k3.

Row 14: K5, p3, k3, p7, k3, p3, k5.

Row 15: K3, p2, k3, yo, k3, skp, k3, k2tog, k3, yo, k3, p2, k3.

Row 16: K5, p4, k3, p5, k3, p4, k5.

Row 17: K3, p2, k4, yo, k3, skp, k1, k2tog, k3, yo, k4, p2, k3.

Row 18: K5, p5, k3, p3, k3, p5, k5.

Row 19: K3, p2, k5, yo, k3, sl 1, k2tog, psso, k3, yo, k5, p2, k3.

Row 20: K5, p6, k7, p6, k5.

Rep Rows 1–20 for pattern.

BACK

Using size 4 needles, cast on 96 (106, 116, 126) sts. Work K1, p1 ribbing for 5 ½" (14 cm) for all sizes, inc 1 st at end of last row—97 (107, 117, 127) sts.

Change to size 6 needles and work patt as follows:

Row 1: P0 (5, 10, 15), *patt Row 1 on next 29 sts, ** p5, rep from * twice, ending last rep at **, p0 (5, 10, 15).

Row 2: K0 (5, 10, 15), *patt Row 2 on next 29 sts, k5**, rep from * twice, ending last rep at **, k0 (5, 10, 15).

Cont to rep Rows 1 and 2, working patt rows on the 29 sts as established, until 13½ (14, 14½, 15)" [34.5 (35.5, 37, 38) cm] from beg.

Armhole Shape

Bind off 4 (5, 6, 7) sts at beg of next 2 rows. Dec 1 st each side every other row 2 (2, 2, 2) times—85 (93,101, 109) sts. Work even until armhole is 7 ½ (8, 8 ½, 9)" [19 (20.5, 21.5, 23) cm].

Shoulder Shape

Bind off 20 (22, 24, 26) sts at beg of next 2 rows. Bind off rem 45 (49, 53, 57) sts.

Front Note: When a pattern has such a large repeat, it is difficult to just divide it in half for each front, so some adjustments have to be made in side stitches. If at all possible, it is best to place main section of a pattern so that it is not cut off by armhole or neck decreases.

LEFT FRONT

Using size 4 needles, cast on 49 (54, 59, 64) sts. Work K1, p1 ribbing as Back, inc 1 st at end of last row—50 (55, 60, 65) sts. Change to size 6 needles and work patt as follows:

Row 1 (RS): K0 (5, 10, 15), k3, p5, patt Row 1 on next 29, p5, k8.

Row 2: P5, k3, k5, patt Row 2 on next 29, k5, k3, p0 (5, 10, 15).

Cont to rep Rows 1 and 2 above for Left Front, working patt rows on the 29 sts as established, until same as Back to armhole, ending at arm side.

Armhole Shape

Bind off 4 (5, 6, 7) sts at beg of next row, cont in patt to end of row. Making sure to keep patt as established, dec 1 st at arm side every other row 2 (2, 2, 2) times—44 (48 52, 56) sts. Work even until armhole is 5 ½ (6, 6 ½, 7)" [14 (15, 16.5, 18) cm], ending at neck edge.

Neck Shape

Bind off 18 (20, 22, 24) sts at beg of next row, then cont in patt to end of row. Making sure to keep patt as established, cont to dec 1 st at neck edge every other row 6 (6, 6, 6) times. Work even until same as Back to shoulder. Bind off rem 20 (22, 24, 26) sts.

RIGHT FRONT

Using size 4 needles, cast on 49 (54, 59, 64) sts. Work K1, p1 ribbing as Back, inc 1 st at end of last row—50 (55, 60, 65) sts. Change to size 6 needles and work patt as follows:

Row 1 (RS): K8, p5, patt Row 1 on next 29, p5, k3, k0 (5, 10, 15).

Row 2: P0 (5, 10, 15), k3, k5, patt Row 2 on next 29, k5, k3, p5.

Cont to rep Rows 1 and 2 above for Right Front, working patt rows on the 29 sts as established, completing Right Front as for Left front.

SLEEVES (MAKE 2)

Using size 4 needles, cast on 48 (54, 58, 64) sts. Work k1, p1 ribbing as Back, inc 1 st at end of last row—49 (55, 59, 65) sts. Change to size 6 needles and work patt as follows:

Row 1 (RS): K2 (5, 7, 10), k3, p5, patt Row 1 on next 29 sts, p5, k3, k2 (5, 7, 10).

Row 2: P2 (5, 7, 10), k3, k5, patt Row 2 on next 29 sts, k5, k3, p2 (5, 7, 10).

Cont to rep Rows 1 and 2 above, working patt rows on the 29 sts as established, inc 1 st each side every 1"(2.5 cm) 7 (8, 9, 10) times—63 (71, 77, 85) sts. Work even until sleeve is 16 (16, 17, 17)" [40.5 (40.5, 43, 43) cm] from beg.

Cap Shape

Bind off 4 (5, 6, 7) sts at beg of next 2 rows. Making sure to keep patt as established, dec 1 st each side every other row 11 (12, 13, 14) times—33 (37, 39, 43) sts. Bind off 2 sts at beg of next 4 rows. Bind off rem 25 (29, 31, 35) sts.

HOOD

With size 4 needles, cast on 106 sts for all sizes. Work k1, p1 ribbing for 1" (2.5 cm), inc 1 st at end of last row—107 sts. Change to size 6 needles and work patt same as for Back Medium size until 13" (33 cm) from beg. Bind off 34 sts at beg of next 2 rows. Keeping center sts in patt as established, work for 5" (12.5 cm) more. Bind off.

FINISHING

Sew shoulder seams. Mark center of Sleeve cap and pin to shoulder seam. Pin armhole bound-off edges of Sleeve cap to armhole edges of Back and Front. Ease Sleeve cap in place, pin, and sew. Sew underarm Sleeve and body seams.

Sew top of Hood seams. Mark center back of Hood and center back of neck. Pin Hood in place starting at front edges, then sew Hood in place.

Fronts and Hood Border (made all in one piece)

With RS facing you, starting at bottom Right Front, pick up 110 (110, 126, 126) sts from bottom to neck-line, pick up 70 sts along right side of Hood, pick up 34 sts along center top of Hood, pick up 70 sts along left side of Hood, pick up 110 (110, 126, 126) sts along Left Front to bottom—394 (394, 426, 426) sts. Knit 4 rows. Bind off loosely.

Prepare Zipper: Work a Blanket Stitch as show on Page 85 on each side of zipper. Pin zipper to Fronts, using the Woven Seam as shown on page 79, sew zipper in place.

Blocking: Lay garment flat on a padded surface, sprinkle with water, pat into shape. Steaming is not recommended for this pattern.

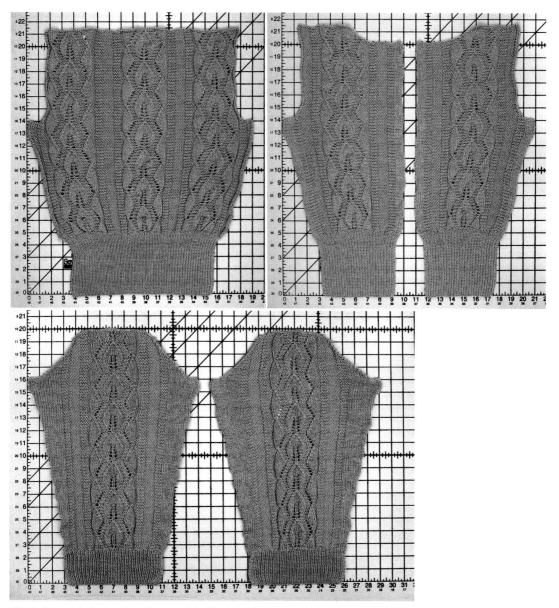

Classic Rectangle body type: pieces on blocking board

Back view of hoodie

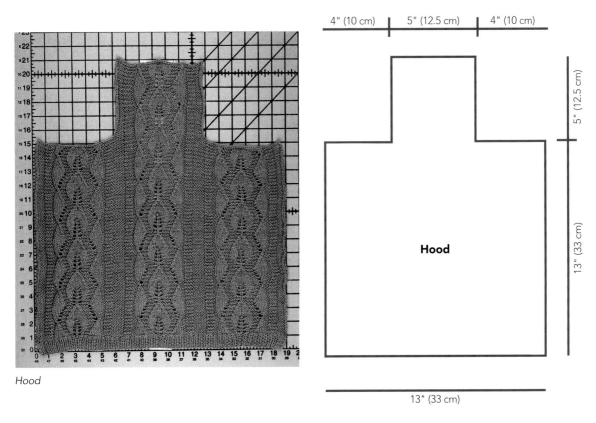

Hood

| 4" (10 cm) | 5" (12.5 cm) | 4" (10 cm) |

5" (12.5 cm)

Hood

13" (33 cm)

13" (33 cm)

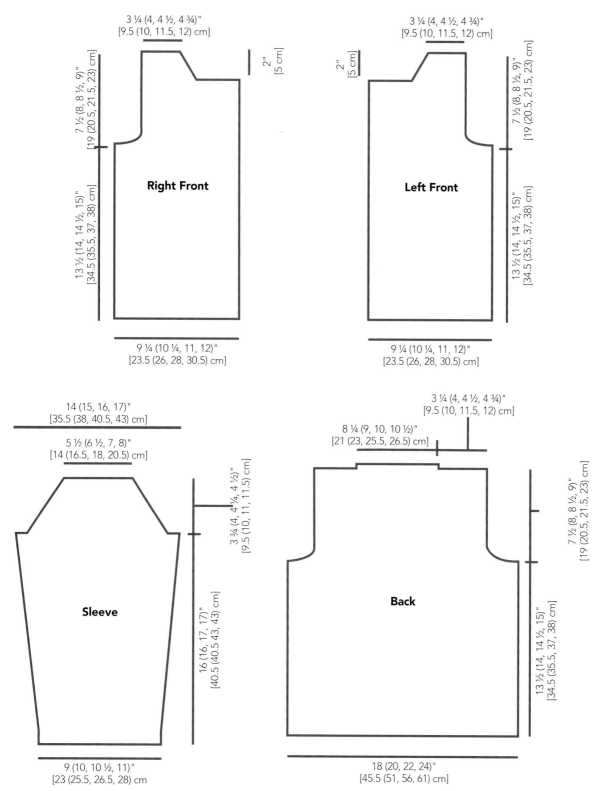

3 ¼ (4, 4 ½, 4 ¾)"
[9.5 (10, 11.5, 12) cm]

2"
[5 cm]

7 ½ (8, 8 ½, 9)"
[19 (20.5, 21.5, 23) cm]

Right Front

13 ½ (14, 14 ½, 15)"
[34.5 (35.5, 37, 38) cm]

9 ¼ (10 ¼, 11, 12)"
[23.5 (26, 28, 30.5) cm]

3 ¼ (4, 4 ½, 4 ¾)"
[9.5 (10, 11.5, 12) cm]

2"
[5 cm]

7 ½ (8, 8 ½, 9)"
[19 (20.5, 21.5, 23) cm]

Left Front

13 ½ (14, 14 ½, 15)"
[34.5 (35.5, 37, 38) cm]

9 ¼ (10 ¼, 11, 12)"
[23.5 (26, 28, 30.5) cm]

14 (15, 16, 17)"
[35.5 (38, 40.5, 43) cm]

5 ½ (6 ½, 7, 8)"
[14 (16.5, 18, 20.5) cm]

3 ¾ (4, 4 ¼, 4 ½)"
[9.5 (10, 11, 11.5) cm]

Sleeve

16 (16, 17, 17)"
[40.5 (40.5 43, 43) cm]

9 (10, 10 ½, 11)"
[23 (25.5, 26.5, 28) cm

3 ¼ (4, 4 ½, 4 ¾)"
[9.5 (10, 11.5, 12) cm]

8 ¼ (9, 10, 10 ½)"
[21 (23, 25.5, 26.5) cm]

7 ½ (8, 8 ½, 9)"
[19 (20.5, 21.5, 23) cm]

Back

13 ½ (14, 14 ½, 15)"
[34.5 (35.5, 37, 38) cm]

18 (20, 22, 24)"
[45.5 (51, 56, 61) cm]

Customize the Fit

THE TRIANGLE

If your body type is Triangle, begin your garment following a size that fits your hip measurement, then gradually decrease to fit the waist and chest measurements of a smaller size. Once you have reached your chest measurement, finish the garment following the smaller size instructions.

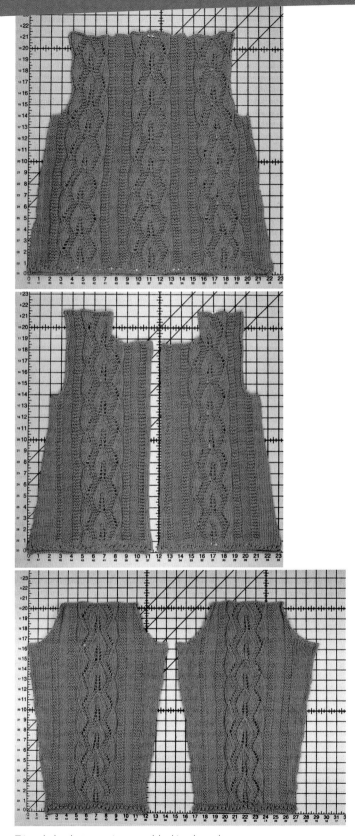

Triangle body type: pieces on blocking board

Customize the Style

To customize the style of this sweater, omit bottom and sleeve ribbed borders and starting with the size #6 knitting needles, work Picot Hem borders (page 99), instead. Work same border around neckline. Embroider flowers and knots (page 108) on Fronts using different colored yarn.

Button Loop: Make an EZ cord (page 107) cast on 20 sts, k1 row, bind off.

Sew cord to top of Right side, forming a loop, sew half-inch (1.3 cm) button to top of Left.

THE INVERTED TRIANGLE

If your body type is Inverted Triangle, begin your garment following a size that fits your hip measurement, then gradually increase to the waist and chest measurement of a larger size. Once you have reached your chest measurement, finish the garment following the larger size instructions.

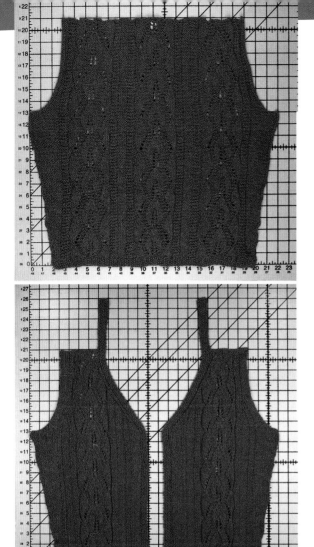

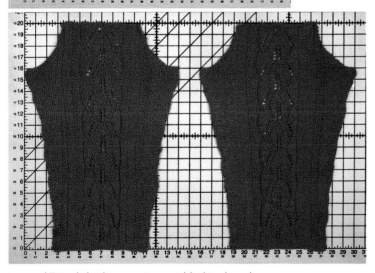

Inverted Triangle body type: pieces on blocking board

Customize the Style

Notions: *Five ½" (1.3 cm) buttons*

To customize this style of sweater, use seed stitch for all the borders, rather than ribbing. Add 5 sts to each Front Edge for a button band and follow directions for seed stitch button band as for Pineapple Twist Rectangle (page 43).

V neck Front: *To shape a V neck, start shaping at the same time armhole shaping is started. Dec 1 stitch at each neck edge every other row, making decreases before or after the seed stitch border. Continue to decrease in this manner, making sure to keep pattern as established, until same amount of shoulder stitches remain, plus 5 seed stitch border stitches. Bind off shoulders, continue on the 5 seed stitches for back neck border, until tab reaches half way across back of neck, bind off. Sew shoulder seams, sew seed stitch tab to back of neck, sew short ends to each other. Sew on buttons.*

THE HOURGLASS

If your body type is Hourglass, begin your garment following a size that fits your hip measurement, then gradually decrease to your waist measurement, work about 2" (5 cm) even, then gradually increase to your chest measurement. Once you have reached your chest measurement, finish the garment following the size that fits your chest measurement.

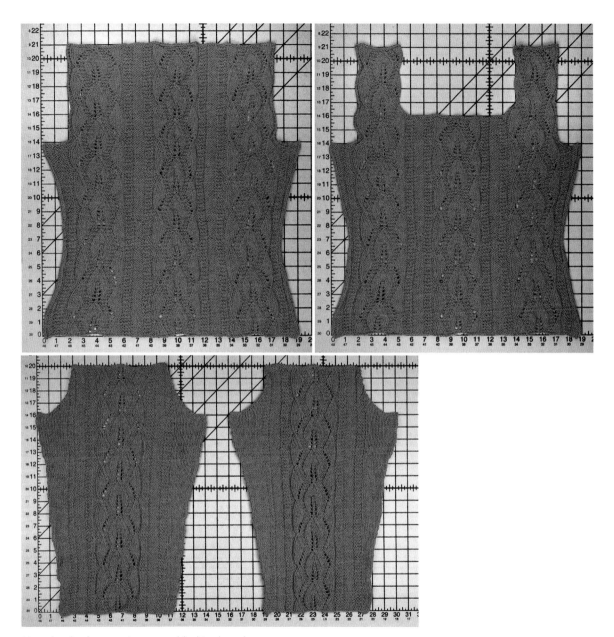

Hourglass body type: pieces on a blocking board

Customize the Style

Pico Hem around neckline

To customize the style of this sweater, we made it into a pullover and eliminated all borders. Begin by using the #6 needles and go right into the pattern. Make the Front the same as Back until the armhole is 3½ (4, 4½, 5)" [7.5 (10,11.5,12.5) cm]. Shape Neck as follows:

Work across 20 (22, 24, 26) sts, join a new ball of yarn, bind off center 45 (49, 53, 57) sts, work remaining 20 (22, 24, 26) sts. Being sure to keep patt as established, working each side on separate ball of yarn, work till same as Back to shoulder, bind off.

Neckband: Sew Shoulder Seams. Starting at Right shoulder, right side facing you, and using a circular # 4 needle, pick up 45 (49, 53, 57) sts across back of neck, pick up 16 sts left side, pick up 45, (49, 53, 57)

Drop Stitch Edging forms a gentle, lacy ruffle

sts across center front, pick up 16 sts on right side of neck—122 (130, 138, 146) sts. Work Picot Hem (page 99).

Sleeve and Bottom Borders: With a #6 needle, make 3 pieces of Leaf Edge Trim (page 102), to fit around bottom and each sleeve. Sew short ends to each other, pin in place, and sew to sweater.

Professional Finishes

High quality finishing work is essential to the success of any project.
Ideally, the inside of your garment can be nearly as neat as the outside.
There are various ways to sew seams, sew on buttons, finish off an edge,
and block your projects. This section shows methods for each of these
finishing steps. Learning these techniques and knowing when to use
them will help you finish your knitted garments like a pro.

Good Habits

Let's begin with a few important practices that will help you knit professional-looking garments.

TEST YOUR GAUGE

Making a gauge swatch before starting your project is so important that failing to do it pretty much guarantees failure of the project.

In order to knit a garment that looks like the project shown, and matches the finished measurements given in the instructions, it is important to choose a yarn in the weight specified in the pattern. This is the first requirement to getting the proper gauge for your project. Gauge refers to the number of stitches and the number of rows in a given width and length, usually over 4" (10 cm) of knitted fabric. The needle size recommended is the size an average knitter would use to get the correct gauge. We can't all be average. Some of us knit tighter, some looser. Before beginning to knit a project, it is very important to take the time to check your gauge. To check your gauge, use the yarn and needle called for in the instructions to cast on the number of stitches indicated by the gauge in the pattern plus at least four more stitches. For example, if the gauge is 16 stitches = 4" (10 cm), cast on at least 20 stitches. Work the pattern stitch until you have knitted a swatch larger than 4" (10 cm) square. Lay the swatch flat and place a ruler over 16 stitches. If there are 16 stitches in 4" (10 cm), you are knitting to the correct gauge. If there are fewer stitches than 16 stitches, you need to use a smaller needle; if there are more than 16, you need to use a larger needle. Don't try to change your personal knitting style; just change your needle size and knit another swatch.

BECOME A ROW COUNTER

Measuring carefully as you work is important, and learning to count rows is another way to contribute to the success of your finished piece. For example, perhaps your instructions tell you to work until the piece measures 11" (28 cm) from the bottom to the armhole, shape the armhole, then work 7½" (19 cm) to the shoulder, shape shoulder, and fasten off. When you knit the fronts, rather than rely on measuring alone, knit the same number of rows for each section. In this way, when you are ready to sew the pieces together, they will match up row for row and the seams will lie flat and even. Counting rows ensures that the sleeves will be the same length; and the fronts will match perfectly.

JOINING NEW YARN

Whenever possible, join new balls of yarn at the beginning of a row. This makes it easy to weave yarn tails into seams when the garment is sewn together. If joining mid-row is unavoidable, try joining in an inconspicuous spot. Loosely tie in the new yarn and finish the row. Work one more row, untie the knot, and retie it to match the gauge of stitches in the previous row.

WEAVING IN TAILS

Always weave yarn tails back into your work to secure them; NEVER tie knots and trim them short. Thread the yarn tail on a large-eye tapestry needle. The yarn needles with curved tips work especially well. For tails along the sides, cast-on, or bind-off edges of a piece, working from the wrong side, weave the yarn in and out of the edge stitches in one direction and then back again in the row right next to it. For tails in the body of the knitting, from the wrong side, make stitches that echo the path of the knitted stitches; one tail going in one direction and the other tail going in the opposite direction.

Seams

There are several different ways to sew seams. Which method to use is sometimes a matter of preference. Other times one way is better for a certain stitch. You may even use two different methods on the same garment; one to create side seams that lie flat, and a sturdier stitch for setting in a sleeve or sewing a shoulder seam. Pinning your pieces together before starting to sew helps keep them even as you work.

The order in which the seams are sewn is also important. For set-in or drop shoulder sleeves, sew the shoulder seams first. Then sew in the sleeves, and finish by sewing the underarm sleeve and side seams. For a garment with raglan sleeves or saddle shoulders, there are no shoulder seams; sew sleeves above the armholes to the garment fronts and backs. The top of the sleeve becomes part of the neckline.

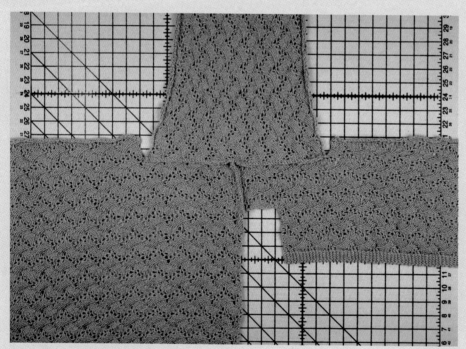

Sew the shoulder seam first; then sew in the sleeve.

MATTRESS STITCH

This invisible seaming stitch is especially useful for joining side seams on sweaters. Lay the pieces edge to edge, right side up. Hook the threaded tapestry needed under the first two running yarns between the selvage and the first column of stitches on one of the pieces. Then, insert your needle under the first two running yarns of the other piece. Zigzag back and forth, catching every two rows in turn. After every few stitches, gently pull the yarn to bring the edges together.

WOVEN SEAM

Use this method for a very flat seam. When done properly, you will not even see your stitches. Hold the pieces to be seamed side by side and, working from the wrong side, insert the needle from front to back through one loop only, draw the yarn through and progress to the next stitch, bring needle through (not over) from back to front, and proceed in this manner until the seam is completed. If you draw the yarn through the top loop only, a decorative ridge will be left on the right side of work. If you draw through bottom loops, the ridge of the seam will be on the inside (wrong side) of the work.

BACKSTITCH SEAM

The backstitch seam works well for joining a set-in sleeve. This method does have some internal bulk, but if done properly, it is strong and helps shape the seam cap nicely. The backstitch method is also a good choice for joining shaped edges. This seam is worked with the right sides together.

Backstitch is a sturdy seam that helps the armhole hold its shape.

Attaching Sleeves

Take care when sewing the sleeves to your garment. The sleeves should fit the armhole smoothly, without puckering, and hang straight, centered in the armhole.

To attach sleeves, first sew the shoulder seams. Then mark the center of the sleeve cap, and pin the sleeve in place, matching the center of the cap to the shoulder seam. Ease the sleeve to fit, pinning the edges together from the center to the underarms. Sew the sleeves in place, using the backstitch seam for set-in sleeves (where the seam is at the crown of the shoulder). Use a more invisible, flat seaming method for sewing drop shoulder sleeves in place.

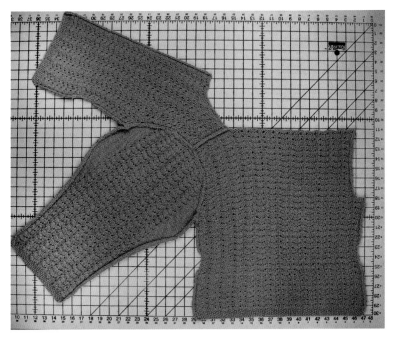

Sleeves being attached on a blocking board.

Collars and Neckbands

Most collars on knitted garments are either made separately and sewn on or picked up and knitted along the front, neck, and back edges, usually on a smaller needle than the body of the garment. Neckbands are usually picked up and worked in same manner. This is necessary for good fit in the neck area, as we usually start shaping the front several inches below the back of neck, making a curve or a V shape to fit the neck.

Front Borders

The front borders, or button/buttonhole bands, on a cardigan are a visual focal point, so it is crucial that they look flawless. Sometimes they are knitted in while you work the fronts, sometimes stitches are picked up and worked after garment is completed, sometimes they are sewn in place.

PICKING UP STITCHES

Knit stitches are wider than they are tall, so when picking up stitches on row ends, the general rule of thumb is to pick up three stitches for every four rows. This guideline works for most people, and your pattern will advise how many stitches to pick up. I like to divide the front in four sections and pick up an equal number of stitches in each section.

You can pick up stitches along an edge with your knitting needle, but I find it much easier to do with a crochet hook of the same size. Then simply transfer the stitches from the hook to your needle.

Single crochet

Reverse single crochet

CROCHET BORDERS

Sometimes a crocheted border can add textural interest to a sweater, such as for the Traveling Vines Cardigan on page 38. Here are basic instructions for the two stitches used, single crochet and reverse single crochet.

Single Crochet. Insert the hook into the specified stitch, wrap the yarn over the hook, and draw the yarn through the stitch so there are 2 loops on the hook (1). Wrap the yarn over the hook again and draw the yarn through both loops (2). When working in single crochet, always insert the hook through both top loops of the next stitch, unless the directions specify front loop or back loop only.

Reverse Single Crochet. At the end of a row, chain 1 but do not turn. Working backward, insert the hook into the previous stitch (1), wrap the yarn over the hook, and draw the yarn through the stitch so there are 2 loops on the hook. Wrap the yarn over the hook again and draw the yarn through both loops. Continue working in the reverse direction (2).

Picking up stitches to crochet

Inserting Zippers

Zippers should always be inserted into knitted garments by hand.

METHOD 1

To ensure that the sides will match, first baste the two sides of the garment together. Center the closed zipper face down over the "seam" on the wrong side of the garment, and pin it in place. Using sewing thread and needle, hand stitch the zipper to the sweater along the outer edges of the zipper tape (1). When complete, remove the basting stitches. (2)

METHOD 2

Before inserting the zipper into the sweater, first prepare the zipper tape with a yarn edging.

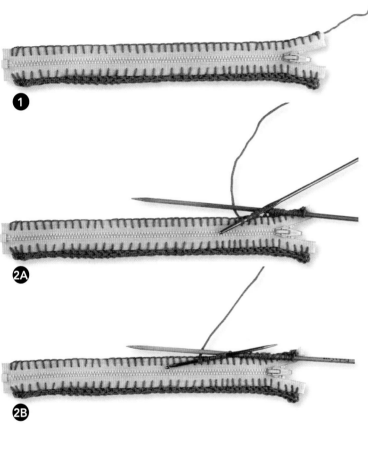

1. Using a sharp, large-eyed hand needle and lightweight yarn or cotton cord, work blanket stitch on both sides of zipper. It helps to measure and mark evenly spaced dots along each side first. If you find the stitching difficult, use an awl to poke holes at the marks.

2A. Using a crochet hook, pick up a loop in each blanket stitch and transfer the stitches to a knitting needle.

2B. Another tool for picking up the stitches has a crochet hook at one end and a knitting needle at the other end.

3. When all stitches are picked up and on the knitting needle, knit one row, then bind off.

Pockets

Add pockets to any of the sweaters, following these instructions. Both styles are fairly inconspicuous, but they may add visual weight to the lower third of the sweater, which can be beneficial for an inverted triangle body type.

PATCH POCKETS

To add a Patch Pocket, decide how wide you want the pocket to be, cast on and work in same pattern as the sweater for about 4 or 5 inches, work 1 inch of a border such as ribbing or seed stitch, bind off. Pin pocket in place on Front of sweater and sew in place.

INSERTED POCKETS

Adding inserted pockets is a little trickier. First start with a pocket lining in plain stockinette stitch. Cast on as many stitches as needed to get the width of the pocket that you would like, work for 4 or 5 inches (10 or 12.5 cm), do not bind off, set aside (1). Begin sweater front, work 4 or 5 inches (10 or 12.5 cm) above bottom border (2). At this point decide where the pocket will be placed on front, work beginning stitches, place marker, work across the same amount of stitches as pocket lining, place these stitches on a holder, work rem sts (3). Next row, work beginning stitches, knit pocket lining in place of the stitches on holder, work remaining stitches, continuing in pattern (4). When front is finished, sew pocket lining to inside of sweater (5). Put stitches on holder back on needle and knit a border of ribbing or seed stitch, for ½" (1.3 cm), bind off. Sew border to sweater at ends.

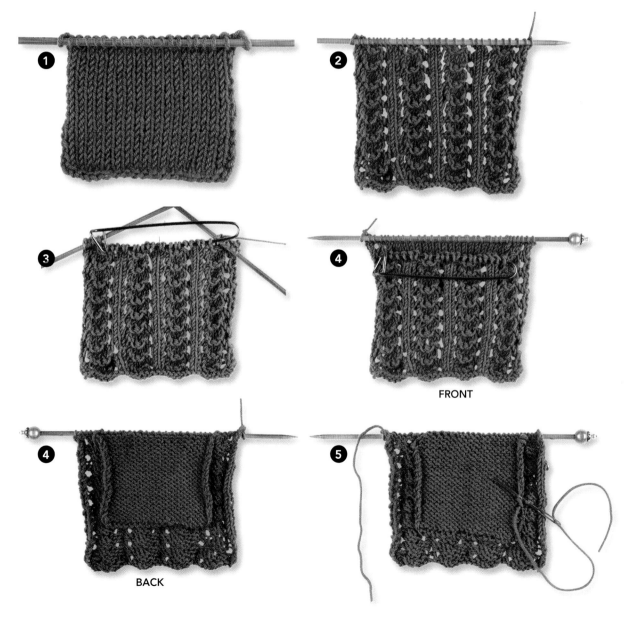

FRONT

BACK

Buttonholes

There are several different ways to make buttonholes in a knitted garment. The type of buttonhole that you choose will depend on the garment style, the weight of the yarn, and the size of the button. It is helpful if you buy your buttons before choosing the method for making buttonholes. The buttonholes should be centered on the front band, evenly spaced, and just large enough for the button to slip through.

Two-Row Buttonhole

TWO-ROW BUTTONHOLE

The two-row buttonhole is made by binding off a number of stitches on the first row and casting them on again on the next row. The cable cast-on makes the neatest edge on the upper part of the buttonhole. The photo shows a two-row buttonhole done in seed stitch, but this buttonhole can be done in many other stitch patterns.

Row 1: Work to the buttonhole placement, knit two, with the left needle pull first stitch over the second stitch (one stitch bound off) *knit 1, pull the second stitch over the knit one, rep from * twice more. Four stitches have been bound off.

Row 2: Work to the bound-off stitches, turn your work, cast on four stitches, using cable cast on method, turn back, finish row. On the next row, work the cast on stitches through the loops to tighten them.

YARN OVER BUTTONHOLES

The Yarn Over buttonholes are small and ideal for small buttons, especially for children's garments. Work as follows to create this buttonhole.

Row 1: Work to the buttonhole placement, yarn over, knit two together, complete row.

Row 2: Work the yarn over as a stitch to complete buttonhole.

The Double Yarn Over Buttonhole

THE DOUBLE YARN OVER BUTTONHOLE

Similar to Yarn over buttonhole, but creates a little larger buttonhole.

Row 1: Work to the buttonhole placement, yarn over twice, knit two together through back loops, finish row.

Row 2: Work to the yarn overs, purl the first yarn over, drop the second yarn over from needle, finish row.

ONE-ROW BUTTONHOLE

The horizontal one-row buttonhole is a very neat buttonhole, and is nicely reinforced and holds its shape.

Row 1: Work to the buttonhole placement, bring yarn to front and slip a stitch as if to purl. Place yarn at back and leave it there. *Slip next stitch from left needle, pass the first slipped stitch over it, repeat from the * three times more (not moving yarn). Slip the last bound-off stitch to left needle and turn work.

Row 2: Using the cable cast-on, with the yarn at back, cast on five stitches, turn the work.

Row 3: Slip the first stitch with the yarn in back from the left needle and pass the extra cast-on stich over it to close the buttonhole. Work to end of row.

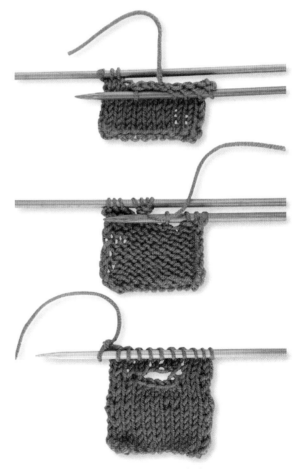

One-Row Buttonhole

Blocking

Many knitters dislike the blocking step as much as they dislike making a gauge swatch. But both steps are crucial to the final fit and appearance of a sweater.

The two main ways of blocking are wet blocking or steam blocking. Because steam blocking involves heat, do not use this method on yarn that contains synthetic fibers. Some like to block each piece before sewing together, some prefer to sew first, then block the finished garment. Either way is fine.

There are a few things that you need for successful blocking. A blocking board with a grid of inches (centimeters) marked out is an invaluable tool. If you do not have a blocking board, you can create a padded surface just about anywhere, by using several towels. You also need a good measuring tape, rust-proof pins, and a pressing cloth if you use the steam method.

WET BLOCKING 1

1. Place the finished garment or pieces on a blocking board or a padded surface, and pin to the desired measurements specified in the schematic or adjusted to fit your body measurements.

2. Wet the pieces with a spray bottle, and pat gently into shape.

3. Allow to dry completely, at least 24 hours.

WET BLOCKING 2

1. Immerse the finished garment or pieces in cool water. Gently squeeze out as much water as possible, but avoid twisting or wringing the piece.

2. Place pieces on a towel, then roll up the towel to remove as much water as possible.

3. Spread the piece to the desired measurements specified in the schematic or adjusted to fit your body measurements, and pin.

4. Allow to dry completely.

STEAM BLOCKING

1. Place the finished garment or pieces on a blocking board or a padded surface, and pin to the desired measurements specified in the schematic or adjusted to fit your body measurements.

2. Spread a dampened pressing cloth over your pieces. Hover a steam iron or handheld steamer over the pressing cloth, but do not press down on the cloth. Allow the steam to penetrate until the fabric is damp.

3. Allow to dry completely.

Oops! How Do I Fix That?

Sometimes, when a garment is totally finished you will realize that everything is not quite as it should be. The edges may not be even or your sleeves may be too long. Sometimes something may happen later on, after the garment has been happily worn. For instance, a snag occurs, or a pet chews a hole in a favorite sweater. Here are a few tricks that can fix some common problems.

DROOPY SHOULDERS

If you have narrow shoulders, and your garment has stretched in the shoulder area, or perhaps you would just like to stabilize that area to prevent stretching, there are two ways to correct this.

You can sew lace seam binding along the top back from shoulder to shoulder as shown.

If you are familiar with crochet, you can work 1 row of slip stitches from the end of one shoulder seam, across the back neck to the end of the other shoulder seam.

SHOULDER PADS

Sometimes small shoulder pads can help balance narrow shoulders and wider hips for the triangular body type. Here's how to make shoulder pads:

1. Knit a small square, using the same yarn as your garment.

2. Fold the square diagonally forming a triangle. Stitch the open edges together.

3. Center the pad over the shoulder seam with the long edge along the sleeve seam and the square corner pointing toward the neckline. Tack the pad in place along the shoulder seam.

TOO ROOMY

You have finished your garment and are so disappointed as it is a bit too big, or the upper arm is too wide. If your yarn is not too bulky, it is possible to take in a seam. This works well if you only need to take in up to one inch. Undo the original seam, sew a new seam to the size that you need, fold the extra fabric to the inside and tack in place. Steam gently.

DROPPED STITCH

You have dropped a stitch, and it is causing a run in your work. A crochet hook is your best friend. Place the head of the crochet hook in the dropped stitch, and loop it up in the next vertical bar, keep doing this until you reach the knitting needle and place the last loop back on the needle.

Pay close attention to whether each row should be knitted or purled. If it should be purled, remove the hook and catch it again from the wrong side.

SHORTENING A GARMENT

You have finished your garment and you find it is too long or the sleeves are too long. You can shorten it by cutting off the bottom and re-knitting the border. When you cut, keep in mind that you will be knitting back several inches (centimeters) for a new border.

Begin by snipping a stitch at the side of work. With right side facing you, unravel a stitch, place your knitting needle in the live stitch, keep unraveling a stitch at a time, catching stitches on the needle as you work across row. When all stitches are on the needle, you can start re-knitting your border.

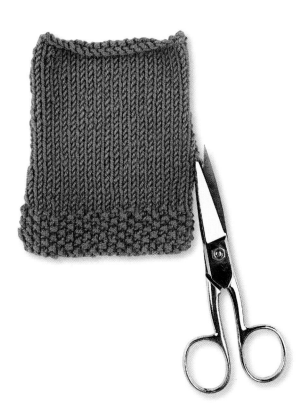

Stylish Embellishments

Embellishing a finished garment can mean anything from adding a simple Picot edge border in place of ribbing, to adding ruffles and lace trims, to appliqueing some motifs around a neckline and or sleeves. There are some examples of how to do this on the garments shown, but there are many other possibilities. You can also add beads and touches of embroidery for an elegant look. Have fun, experiment, and make every garment special.

Decorative Edges

1 X 1 RIB

Cast on an odd number of stitches.

Row 1: K1, *p1, k1, rep from * across row.

Row 2: P1, *k1, p1, rep from * across row.

Rep Rows 1 and 2 for pattern.

2 X 2 RIB

Cast on a multiple of 4 plus 2.

Row 1: K2, *p2, k2, rep from * across row.

Row 2: P2, *k2, p2, rep from * across row.

Rep Rows 1 and 2 for pattern.

MISTAKE STITCH RIBBING

Cast on a multiple of 4 plus 3.

Note: This pattern is called Mistake Stitch because it doesn't follow the expected rib procedure. When the pattern begins to emerge, you will see it clearly.

Row 1: *K2, p2, rep from * to last 3 sts, end k2, p1.

Rep Row 1 for pattern.

BI-OR SAND STITCH

Notes: *Made with 2 ors, A and B. Do not cut yarn at end of rows, carry up sides as you work.*

Cast on a multiple of 2 plus 1.

Row 1: (RS): With A, knit.

Row 2: With A, knit.

Row 3: With B, k1, *sl 1 pwise, k1, rep from * across row.

Row 4: With B, k1, *yarn forward (yf), sl 1 pwise, yarn back (yb), k1, rep from * across row.

Rep Rows 1–4 for pattern.

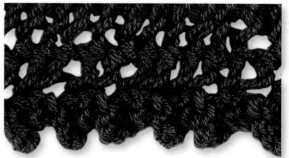

MOCK CABLE RIB

Cast on a multiple of 4 plus 2.

Row 1 (WS): K2, *p2, k2, rep from * across row.

Row 2: P2, *k1, yo, k1, p2, rep from * across row.

Row 3: K2, *p3, k2, rep from * across row.

Row 4: P2, *sl 1, k2, psso both k sts, p2, rep from * across row.

Rep Rows 1–4 for pattern.

LACY PICO I

Foundation Row: Cast on 7 sts, knit one row.

Row 1: K1, k2tog, yo twice, k2tog, yo twice, k2.

Row 2: Sl 1, k1, (k1, p1) into large yo loop formed by the 2 yo's, k1, (k1, p1) into large yo loop formed by the 2 yo's, k2.

Row 3: K1, k2tog, yo twice, k2tog, k4.

Row 4: Bind off 2 sts, k2, (k1, p1) into large yo loop formed by the 2 yo's, k2.

Rep Rows 1 through 4 for desired length, bind off.

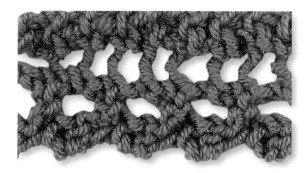

LACY PICO II

Foundation Row: Cast on 7 sts, knit one row.

Row 1: Sl 1, k1, yo, k2tog, yo, k2tog, k1.

Row 2: Rep Row 1.

Row 3: Rep Row 1 until last st, k in front, back and front of last st (beginning of picot).

Row 4: SKP (sl 1 st, k next st, pass sl st over the k st), k1, pass the first st over to complete the picot, k1, yo, k2tog, yo, k2tog, k1.

Rep Rows 1 through 4 for desired length, bind off.

EYELET LACE

Note: For this pattern, yarn overs are made by wrapping yarn from front, back over needle, front again.

Pick up or cast on a multiple of 4.

Row 1: P2 *yo, P4tog, * rep from * end p2.

Row 2: K2 * k1, work (k1, p1, k1) into the yo space, rep from *, end k2.

Row 3: Knit.

Repeat Rows 1–3 for pattern.

TIC-TAC-TOE

Notes: *Yarn overs (yo) throughout this pattern are always made wrapping yarn twice around needle.*

Worked with 2 ors, A and B.

With A, cast on a multiple of 5 plus 1.

Row 1: Purl.

Row 2: Knit.

Row 3: P1, *yo, p3, yo, p2, rep from * to end.

Row 4: With B, k1, sl 1, dropping extra wrap, k2, sl 1 dropping extra wrap, *[k1, yo, k1, yo, k1] into the next st (starting bobble st), sl 1 dropping extra wrap, k2, sl 1 dropping extra wrap, rep from * to last st, end k1.

Row 5: P1, sl 1, p2, sl 1, *yarn back (yb), k5, yarn front (yf), sl 1, p2, sl 1, rep from * to last st, end p1.

Row 6: K1, sl 1, k2, sl 1, *yf, p5, yb, sl 1, k2, sl 1, rep from * to last st, end k1.

Row 7: P1, sl 1, p2, sl 1, *yb, k2tog, k3tog, pass the k2tog st over the k3tog st, yf, sl 1, p2, sl 1, rep from * to last st, end p1.

Row 8 (Cross Row): With A k1, *drop the first long loop off the needle, with yb, sl 2, drop next long loop off needle, with left-hand needle pick up the first dropped long loop, pass the 2 slipped sts from right-hand needle back to left-hand needle, then pick up the second dropped long loop, k5 (you will be knitting a long loop, 2 sts in between, second long loop, and the ending bobble stitch), rep from * to end.

Rep Rows 1–3. Bind off.

HYACINTH BORDER

Cast on a multiple of 6 plus 2.

Row 1 (WS): K1 *p3tog, p2tog, pass the p3tog st over the p2tog st, (k1, p1, k1, p1, k1) into the next st, rep from * to last st, end k1.

Rows 2 and 4: K1, p to last st, k1.

Row 3: K1, *(k1, p1, k1, p1, k1) into the next st, p3tog, p2tog, pass the p3tog st over the p2tog st, rep from * to last st, end k1.

Row 5: K1, k across, wrapping yarn 3 times around needle for each st to last st, end k1.

Row 6: K1, p across row, dropping extra loops off needle to last st, end k1.

Rep Rows 1–6 for pattern.

Picot Hem

PICOT HEM

A picot hem is a lovely way to finish a garment. The yarn over row creates little holes that become dainty picots when the hem is turned to the inside along this row and sewn down.

Rows 1 and 3: Knit.

Rows 2 and 4: Purl.

Row 5: K1, *yarn over, k2tog, repeat from * across row.

Rows 6 and 8: Purl.

Row 7: Knit.

Bind off. Fold to inside of garment at yarn over row, forming little points, sew to inside of garment.

Note: *If hem is worked in the round, knit every row.*

DROP STITCH EDGING

This border can be worked at the beginning of a garment, or it can be knitted separately and sewn on later. One important thing to remember when working this pattern at the beginning of a project is that, one third of the stitches are going to be dropped, so cast on an extra third to compensate for this.

Row 1: K1 from back (K1b) *p2, k1b, rep from * across row.

Row 2: P1, *k1b, k1, p1, rep from * across row.

Rep Rows 1 and 2 for desired length.

Next row: K1b, *drop next st off needle, p1, k1b, rep from * across.

Work the next 2 rows in ribbing as follows:

Row 1: P1, *k1b, p1, rep from * across row.

Row 2: K1b, *p1, k1b, rep from * across.

At this point border may be bound off. If you are continuing on a project, you may have to increase or decrease a stitch or two to meet the multiple of the pattern that you choose to work.

Drop Stitch Edging

OPENWORK BELL

This edging is worked side to side, it may be made separately and sewn onto bottom or sleeve edges or it may be worked at the beginning of a garment. About two thirds of the stitches are decreased from the cast on edge, so this must be taken into consideration when beginning. Stitches may be increased or decreased on last row to adjust to your pattern.

Multiple of 14 plus 3

Row 1 (RS): Knit.

Row 2: Knit.

Row 3: P3, *k11, p3, rep from * to end.

Row 4: K3, *p11, k3, rep from * to end.

Row 5: P3, *yb (yarn back), sl 1, k1, psso, k2, yo, sl 1, k2tog, psso, yo, k2, k2tog, p3, rep from * to end.

Row 6: K3, *p9, k3, rep from * to end.

Row 7: P3, *yb, sl 1, k1, psso, k1, yo, sl 1, k2tog, psso, yo, k1, k2tog, p3, rep from * to end.

Row 8: K3, *p7, k3, rep from * to end.

Row 9: P3, *yb, sl 1, k1, psso, yo, sl 1, k2tog, psso, yo, k2tog, p3, rep from * to end.

Row 10: K3, *p5, k3, rep from * to end.

Row 11: P3, *yb, sl 1, k1, psso, k1, k2tog, p3, rep from * to end.

Row 12: K3, *p3, k3, rep from * to end.

Row 13: P3, *yb, sl 1, k2tog, psso, p3, rep from * to end.

Row 14: K3, *p1, k3, rep from * to end.

Row 15: P3, *k1, p3, rep from * to end.

Row 16: Same as row 14.

Bind off if sewing, or adjust stitches and continue with garment.

SMALL BELLS

The textured, open work little bells, make a great edging for children's garments.

Multiple of 8 plus 4

Row 1 (RS): Purl.

Row 2: Knit.

Row 3: P4, *cast on 8 sts, p4, rep from * across row.

Row 4: K4, *p8 (you will be purling the 8 cast on sts), k4, rep from * across row.

Row 5: P4, *k8, p4, rep from * across row.

Row 6: K4, *p8, k4, rep from * across row.

Row 7: P4, *ssk, k4, k2tog, p4, rep from * across row.

Row 8: K4, *p6, k4, rep from * across row.

Row 9: P4, *ssk, k2, k2tog, p4, rep from * across row.

Row 10: K4, *p4, k4, rep from * across row.

Row 11: P4, *ssk, k2tog, p4, rep from * across row.

Row 12: K4, *p2, k4, rep from * across row.

Row 13: P4, *k2tog, p4, rep from * across row.

Row 14: K4, *p1, k4, rep from * across row.

Row 15: P4, *k2tog, p3, rep from * across row.

LARGE BELLS

This edging can be picked up on the bottom edge of a garment or a sleeve edge and worked, or it may be worked separately and sewn on. I like the way it looks from both sides, so pick the side that you like best.

Cast on or pick up a multiple of 6 plus 1.

Row 1–5: Knit.

Row 6 (WS): K3, *p1, k5, rep from *, ending last rep k3.

Row 7: P3, *yo, k1, yo, p5, rep from *, ending last rep p3.

Row 8: K3, *p3, k5, rep from *, ending last rep k3.

Row 9: P3, *yo, k3, yo, p5, rep from *, ending last rep p3.

Row 10: K3, *p5, k5, rep from *, ending last rep k3.

Row 11: P3, *yo, k5, yo, p5, rep from *, ending last rep p3.

Row 12: K3, *p7, k5, rep from *, ending last rep k3.

Row 13: P3, *yo, k7, yo, p5, rep from *, ending last rep p3.

Row 14: K3, *p9, k5, rep from *, ending last rep k3.

Row 15: P3, *yo, k9, yo, p5, rep from *, ending last rep p3.

Row 16: K3, *p11, k5, rep from *, ending last rep k3.

Row 17: P3, *yo, k11, yo, p5, rep from *, ending last rep p3.

Row 18: K3, *p13, k5, rep from *, ending last rep k3.

Row 19: P3, *yo, k13, yo, p5, rep from *, ending last rep p3.

Row 20: K3, *p15, k5, rep from *, ending last rep k3.

Bind off loosely in pattern.

Note: *if you have a tendency to bind off too tight, use a larger needle for bind off).*

ON POINTE

This edging is worked side to side and the stitches that are cast on do not change. It can be worked at the beginning of a garment in place of a more conventional border.

Multiple of 13 plus 1.

Cast on 66 sts.

Rows 1, 3, 5, and 7 (WS): Purl.

Rows 2, 4, and 6: *K1, yo, k4, (k2tog) twice, k4, yo, rep from * across row, end k1.

Rows 8, 9, 10, and 11: Knit all stitches across row.

If stitches have to be adjusted to conform to the body of garment, make adjustments on Row 11.

LACY SCALLOP

Muliple of 13 plus 2.

This edging is worked side to side, so it may be made separately and sewn onto bottom or sleeve edges or it may be worked at the beginning of a garment. About a quarter of the stitches are decreased from the cast on edge, so this must be taken into consideration when beginning. Stitches may be increased or decreased on last row to adjust to your pattern.

Row 1 (RS): K 3, *sl, 1 k1, psso, sl 2, k3tog, p2sso, k2tog, k4, rep from * to last 12 sts, sl 1, k1, psso, sl 2, k3tog, p2sso, k2tog, k3.

Row 2: P4, *yo, p1, yo, p6, rep from * to last 5 sts, yo, p1, yo, p4.

Row 3: K1, yo, *k2, sl 1, k1, psso, k1, k2tog, k2, yo, rep from * to last st, k1.

Row 4: P2, *yo, p2, yo, p3, yo, p2, yo, p1, rep from * to last st, p1.

Row 5: K2, yo, k1, *yo, sl 1, k1, psso, k1, sl 1, k2tog, psso, k1, k2tog, (yo, k1) 3 times, rep from * to last 12 sts, yo, sl 1, k1, psso, k1, sl 1, k2tog, psso, k1, k2tog, yo, k1, yo, k2.

Row 6: Purl.

Row 7: K5, *yo, sl 2, k3tog, p2sso, yo, k7, rep from * to last 10 sts, yo, sl 2, k3tog, p2sso, yo, k5.

Row 8: Knit.

Bind off if sewing, or adjust stitches and continue with garment.

LEAF EDGE TRIM

Cast on 8 sts.

Row 1 (RS): K5, yo, k1, yo, k2.

Row 2: P6, knit into front and back of next st (inc made now and throughout), k3.

Row 3: K4, p1, k2, yo, k1, yo, k3.

Row 4: P8, inc in the next st, k4.

Row 5: K4, p2, k3, yo, k1, yo, k4.

Row 6: P10, inc in the next st, k5.

Row 7: K4, p3, k4, yo, k1, yo, k5.

Row 8: P12, inc in the next st, k6.

Row 9: K4, p4, ssk, k7, k2tog, k1.

Row 10: P10, inc in the next st, k7.

Row 11: K4, p5, ssk, k5, k2tog, k1.

Row 12: P8, inc in the next st, k2, p1, k5.

Row 13: K4, p1, k1, p4, ssk, k3, k2tog, k1.

Row 14: P6, inc in the next st, k3, p1, k5.

Row 15: K4, p1, k1, p5, ssk, k1, k2tog, k1.

Row 16: P4, inc in the next st, k4, p1, k5.

Row 17: K4, p1, k1, p6, sl 1, k2tog, psso, k1.

Row 18: P2tog, bind off next 5 sts, using the stitch made by the p2tog to bind off first st, p3, k4.

Rep Rows 1–8 for Leaf Edge pattern.

GARTER STITCH SCALLOPS

Small scallop, large scallop in ( )

Cast on 3 (7) sts, knit 1 row.

Row 1: K1 (5), inc 1 st in next st, k1 (1).

Row 2: K1 (1) Inc 1 st in the next st, k2 (6).

Row 3: K3 (7), inc 1 st in next st, k1 (1).

Row 4: K1 (1), inc 1 st in next st, k4 (8).

Row 5: K5 (9), inc 1 st in next st, k1 (1).

Row 6: K1 (1), inc 1 st in next st, k6 (10).

Row 7: K7 (11), inc 1 st in next st, k1 (1).

Row 8: K1 (1), inc 1 st in next st, k8 (12).

Row 9: K8 (12), k2tog, k1 (1).

Row 10: K1 (1), k2tog, k7 (11).

Row 11: K6 (10), k2tog, k1 (1).

Row 12: K1 (1), k2tog, k5 (9).

Row 13: K4 (8), k2tog, k1 (1).

Row 14: K1 (1), k2tog, k3 (7).

Row 15: K2 (6), k2tog, k1 (1).

Row 16: K1 (1), k2tog, k1 (5).

Rep Rows 1–16 for desired length.

VERTICAL EYELET LACE

Cast on 7 sts.

Rows 1 and 3: K2, p3, k2.

Rows 2 and 4: K1, p1, k3, p1, k1.

Row 5: K2, p1, yo by wrapping yarn around needle, p2tog, k2.

Row 6: Rep Row 2.

Rep rows 1–6 for desired length.

AIRY GARTER STITCH

Cast on an even number of stitches.

Rows 1–4: Knit.

Row 5 (RS): *K1, yo twice, rep from *, end k1.

Row 6: Knit across row, dropping the extra wraps.

Rows 7–9: Knit.

Bind off.

TRINITY STITCH BORDER

Cast on a multiple 4 plus 2.

Row 1 (RS): K1, purl to last st, k1.

Row 2: K1, *(k1, p1, k1) all in next st, p3tog, rep from * across row to last st, end k1.

Row 3: K1, purl to last st, k1.

Row 4: K1, * p3tog, (k1, p1, k1) all in next st, rep from * across row to last st, end k1.

Rep Rows 1–4 for desired width. Bind off.

Motifs

SMALL LEAF

Ssk: slip 2 sts to right needle as if to knit, slip left needle through front of sts and k2tog through the back loop.

Psso: Pass slipped st over the knit sts.

Cast on 5 sts.

Row 1 (RS): K2, yo, k1, yo, k2 (7 sts).

Row 2 and all even rows: Purl.

Row 3: K3, yo, k1, yo, k3 (9 sts).

Row 5: K4, yo, k1, yo, k4 (11 sts).

Row 7: K5 yo, k1, yo, k5 (13 sts).

Row 9: K6, yo, k1, yo, k6 (15 sts).

Row 11: K1, ssk, k9, k2tog, k1 (13 sts).

Row 13: K1, ssk, k7, k2tog, k1 (11 sts).

Row 15: K1, ssk, k5, k2tog, k1 (9 sts).

Row 17: K1, ssk, k3, k2tog, k1 (7 sts).

Row 19: K1, ssk, k1, k2tog, k1 (5 sts).

Row 21: K1, ssk, k2tog (3 sts).

Row 23: Sl 1, k2tog, psso (1 st).

Bind off rem st.

KNIT FLOWER 1

Cast on 62 sts.

Row 1 (WS): Purl.

Row 2: K2, *k1, sl this st back onto left needle, then lift the next 9 sts on left needle over this st and off the needle, yo, knit the first st again, k2, rep from * (22 sts).

Row 3: P1, *p2tog, k front, back, front in the yo, p1, rep from * to last st, end p1 (27 sts).

Row 4: K1, *sl 2, k1, p2sso, rep from *, end k2 (11 sts).

Row 5: *P2tog, rep from *, end p1 (6 sts).

Row 6: Sl 2nd, 3rd, 4th, 5th and 6th sts over first st. Bind off.

Sew a seam to form flower.

KNIT FLOWER 2

Multiple of 13 plus 1

Cast on 66 sts.

Rows 1, 3, 5 and 7: Purl (wrong side)

Rows 2, 4 and 6: *K1, yo, k4, (k2tog) twice, k4, yo, rep from * across row, end K1.

Row 8: *K2tog, rep from * across row (33 sts).

Row 9: *K2tog, rep from * across row to last st, k1 (17 sts).

Row 10: *K2tog, rep from * across row to last st, k1 (9 sts).

Do not bind off, cut yarn leaving an 18" (45.7 cm) length, thread remaining yarn onto a tapestry needle and draw yarn through live stitches and gather. Reinforce gather by going around again, sew beginning and ending petal together to form flower. Use remaining yarn to attach flower to garment.

SMALL FAN

Worked with 2 colors, A and B.

With A, cast on 26 sts.

Row 1: Knit.

Row 2: K1, *yo, k2tog, rep from *, end k1.

Row 3: Knit.

Row 4: Knit.

Row 5: With B, *k1, sl 1, repeat from * end k2tog.

Row 6: *K1, yarn front (yf), sl 1, yarn back (yb), rep from *, end yb, k1.

Row 7: With A, knit.

Row 8: Knit.

Row 9: With B, * k1, sl 1, rep from *, end k1.

Row 10: Repeat Row 6.

Row 11: With A, knit.

Row 12 (first dec row): K1 *k2tog through back loop, rep from * across (13 sts).

Row 13: With B, *k1, sl 1, rep from * to last st. end k1.

Row 14: Repeat Row 6. Bind off B.

Row 15: With A, knit.

Row 16 (2nd dec row): K1, *k2tog, rep from * across (7 sts).

Row 17: Knit.

Row 18: K2tog, k3, k2tog (5 sts).

Row 19: Knit.

Row 20: K2tog, k1, k2tog (3 sts).

Row 21: Knit.

Row 22: K3tog. Bind off.

Ties

Pull the working yarn tight across the back of the stitches and knit another row. Repeat this many times, forming a narrow knitted tube. To keep the stitches looking uniform, tug on the tube every few rows.

EZ CORD

Another way to knit narrow ties is to simply cast on stitches to the desired length, knit one row, then bind them back off again.

I-CORD

Narrow tubes can be knit using two double-point needles. These tubes are known as idiot cord, or merely I-cord. Any tube that has five stitches or less in circumference can be worked as I-cord.

Cast on or pick up the required number of stitches on a double-pointed needle. Knit the stitches with another double-pointed needle, but don't turn the work. Slide the stitches to the opposite end of the needle.

Embroidery

Embroidering on a knitted sweater is similar to embroidering on woven fabrics, but you typically do not use an embroidery hoop. Thread yarn onto a blunt-end tapestry needle. Avoid piercing the yarn of the sweater; rather insert the needle between yarns in the knit. Weave in ends securely on the back of the sweater.

CROSS STITCH

Use the knit stitches as a guide for making evenly spaced cross stitches of equal size. For the first pass, make all diagonal stitches in one direction. Then cross the stitches in the other diagonal direction on the second pass.

FRENCH KNOTS

Bring the yarn to the front, and pull all the way through. Wrap the needle once, twice, or three times, depending on the desired size. Holding light tension on the yarn where it emerges from the surface, insert the needle back into the fabric in an adjacent hole, not in the same hole. Pull the needle to the back, releasing the yarn and forming the knot.

LAZY DAISY

Bring the needle to the right side and re-insert it to the back in the same hole. As you pull the yarn through, a loop forms on the surface. Bring the needle back to the top through the loop, and cross the top of the loop with a short stitch. Continue in a circle to form a flower.

DUPLICATE STITCH

The results of duplicate stitch embroidery look as if you knitted the or into the sweater. Stitch over the knit stitches, echoing the path of the yarn.

Sweater Gallery

Little Shells

10   18   20   22

Travelling Vines

24   32   35   38

Pineapple Twist

42   49   54   58

Climbing Leaf

60   68   70   72

Classic Rectangle   *Triangle*   *Inverted Triangle*   *Hourglass*

Abbreviations

Here is the list of standard abbreviations used for knitting. Until you can readily identify them, keep the list handy whenever you knit.

beg	begin	pwise	purlwise
bet	between	rep	repeat
BO	bind off	rev St st	reverse stockinette stitch
CC	contrasting or	rib	ribbing
cm	centimeter	rnd(s)	rounds
cn	cable needle	RS	right side
CO	cast on	sk	skip
Col	Color	skp	slip 1, knit 1, pass slipped stitch over (decrease)
cont	continue	sl	slip
dec	decrease	sl1k	slip one knitwise
dpn	double-pointed needle(s)	sl1p	slip one purlwise
g	grams	sl st	slip stitch
inc	increase	sm	slip marker
k	knit	ssk	slip 1, slip 1, knit these 2 stitches together (decrease)
k1f&b	knit into front and back loop of same stitch	st(s)	stitch(es)
k2tog	knit two stitches together	St st	stockinette stitch
kwise	knitwise	tbl	through back loop
m(s)	markers(s)	tog	together
MC	main or	WS	wrong side
rem	remaining or remain	wyb	with yarn in back
rep	repeat	wyf	with yarn in front
mm	millimeters	yb	yarn back
M1	make one stitch (increase)	yf	yarn forward
oz	ounce	yo	yarn over needle
p	purl	*	repeat from *
p1f&b	purl into front and back loop of same stitch	[ ]	repeat instructions in brackets as directed
p2tog	purl two stitches together	( )	repeat instructions in parentheses as directed
patt	pattern	( )	number of stitches that should be on the needle or across a row
pm	place marker		
psso	pass slipped stitch over		